LEADERS ON "UP THE MOOD ELEVATOR"

"Larry Senn has had a profound influence on my life through elegant, yet simple principles, now found in 'Up the Mood Elevator.' Practice the lessons in 'Up the Mood Elevator' and the arc of your life will be changed forever...for the better."

Dr. Gordon Gee
President, The Ohio State University

"Larry Senn has developed an incredibly valuable way to think about culture. At Limited Brands, our thinking, behaviors and results (both hard and soft) have been positively impacted by culture shaping work led by Larry and his team. 'Up the Mood Elevator' inspires leaders to live more of life at their best, build better relationships and create more success."

Leslie H. Wexner
Chairman and CEO, Limited Brands

"Larry's gift of offering simple plus powerful guidance to high happiness and success is masterful. The Mood Elevator tool is helping change lives, organizations and families; thus our world. I invite any leader interested in upping their organization's mood and impact to read 'Up the Mood Elevator.'"

Vance Caesar, PhD
Author of "The High Achievers' Guide to Happiness and Uncommon Career Success"

"This book is the ticket for anyone who wants to spend more time on the top floors of the Mood Elevator. The concept has been invaluable in all walks of life. It helps us work better together as business colleagues, but has equal benefit in personal relationships. There is much to be gained from an attitude of gratitude and understanding how to get there. Larry Senn is doing a great service by bringing the Mood Elevator to a larger audience."

General Josue (Joe) Robles, Jr.
President and CEO, USAA
The number one service company in America

"Larry Senn and the concepts he teaches like the Mood Elevator have had a profound impact on my career, the success of YUM! Brands around the world and on me personally."

David Novak
Chairman and CEO, YUM! Brands
Author of "Taking People with You"
2012 CEO of the Year

"I have been anxiously waiting for Larry's book, 'Up The Mood Elevator.' As his personal physician for decades, I know that Larry has been living the principles of the Mood Elevator and that this has resulted in his phenomenal cardiovascular and mental health. The principles of the Mood Elevator regarding living a balanced life emotionally and physically are cornerstones of cardiovascular risk reduction, as Larry has illustrated personally and in the thousands of people he has influenced through his work."

Jay A. Johnson, MD, FACC
Board Certified Cardiologist
Attending Staff Stanford University Medical Center

"'Up the Mood Elevator–Living Life At Your Best' is a must 'read.' It provides essential information on the impact your own Mood Elevator has on your individual life, your family and friends, and the culture of your organization."

Steve Gabbe, MD
CEO, The Ohio State University Wexner Medical Center

"'Up the Mood Elevator' is an engaging lift into the deeper aspects of our selves and the richest parts of our lives. Through his immense personal and corporate experience, Larry Senn shares practical wisdom on how to enhance our success in business, relationships, health, and everyday living.

In reading some 'self-help' books, I feel as if I'm getting sold a life that isn't mine and steps to get there that if not impossible, are naive and unrealistic. Senn's style in 'Up the Mood Elevator,' helps me to focus on the life I have and the person I am. I no longer want a life that isn't mine, but to live my life more fully."

Reverend Joshua Reeves

"The Mood Elevator is the best thinking and guidance I have ever read on healthy living for individuals and healthy cultures for organizations. The tools are being used and embraced in our organization and we are experiencing remarkable results."

Gary Shorb
CEO, Methodist LeBonheur Healthcare"

"In 'Up the Mood Elevator,' Larry Senn has given leaders a remarkably effective tool to harness the power of introspection to focus on what matters most to their organization's success and to help them be their personal best both in and outside of the office."

Gail K. Boudreaux
CEO, UnitedHealthcare

"It is an amazing book that elevates your moods to the highest levels; and unlocks your potential to achieve all-round success in your life. I wish I had this book long ago."

Professor M.S. Rao,
International Leadership expert,
Author of "Soft Leadership"

"Limited Brands and their Victoria's Secret brand were named the Most Admired Specialty Retailer by Fortune. They also had the highest same store sales gains. Senn Delaney played a role both with the CEO and senior team and by bringing concepts like the Mood Elevator to every store around the world."

Sharen Jester Turney
CEO, Victoria's Secret

"The Mood Elevator had been a tremendous tool in helping our team elevate the energy and commitment to the task at hand."

Mike Glenn
CEO, FedEx Services

"Once again Larry Senn has written a book which is simple to understand but has profound implications on how we interact. He makes the point that we are in control of our mood. I highly recommend this book."

Tom Voss
Chairman, President & CEO, Ameren Corporation

"Larry Senn transforms already hardworking and smart winners and takes them to a much higher level of performance. My personal learning regarding the Mood Elevator and the Shadow I cast on the organization had an immediate and very positive impact on the morale of our executive team."

Ahmad R. Chatila
CEO, MEMC/SunEdison

"'Up the Mood Elevator' is a great book. Reading it has had a profound effect on my life—both business and personal."

Lloyd Greif, President & CEO, Greif & Co.
Lloyd Greif Center for Entrepreneurial Studies
USC Marshall School of Business

"Larry has had a significant impact on me and the way I have managed cultures within the two companies I've been fortunate to lead. His tools for teaching leaders how to doing the "right people" things leave an indelible mark on the emotional IQ of any business enterprise. The Mood Elevator has become an important part of the nomenclature of the companies I've run."

Mark Frissora
Chairman and CEO, The Hertz Corporation

"The book is brilliant! Growing up, the book that influenced me perhaps more than any was Napoleon Hill's 'Think and Grow Rich'. This is really like the modern day version of think and grow rich ... the concept that our thinking creates our feelings makes us realize what control we have. Great stories."

Robert Reiss
Host, The CEO Show

Your guide to success without stress...

Up the Mood Elevator

Living Life At Your Best

Larry Senn

Library of Congress Control Number: 2012918994
Senn, Larry

ISBN-10: 0963601865
ISBN-13: 978-0963601865

First edition, January 2013

Printed in the United States of America

Printing number
1 2 3 4 5 6 7 8 9 0

For more information please visit:
www.upthemoodelevator.com

or contact:
larry@upthemoodelevator.com

This book is dedicated to my wife and soul mate Bernadette and to our five children Kevin, Darin, Jason, Kendra and Logan. You provide the love, purpose, inspiration, perspective, gratitude and life lessons that help me gracefully ride the Mood Elevator of life.

[table of contents]

preface

I invite you to join me on a journey of understanding about a concept that can be life altering – the Mood Elevator. As Gordon Gee, President of The Ohio State University, said "Practice the lessons in Up the Mood Elevator and the arc of your life will be changed forever…for the better."

I had been researching and gathering ideas for this book for several years but had allowed a busy personal and professional life to keep me from completing it. My motivation to complete it came from work I did to clarify my own life purpose in an in-house session on personal purpose we conducted at Senn Delaney for all employees. As I took the time in an off-site to reflect on how I hoped to make a difference in the world, it became clear that my purpose was to "provide understanding and inspiration to an ever widening circle of people, beginning with my family, to live life at their best mentally, emotionally, physically and spiritually." As soon as I articulated that, I knew I needed to complete the book. I saw sharing these ideas with the world as one of the best ways to bring that purpose to life.

You will see 'Senn Delaney' referred to throughout the book. It is a firm I founded over three decades ago to fulfill a vision I had of enhancing the spirit and performance of organizations by systematically shaping their cultures. For those who aren't familiar with the firm, it is widely recognized today as the most successful culture-shaping consulting firm in the world. The

Mood Elevator and its engaging graphic is just one of many concepts used by Senn Delaney as part of its overall process to create thriving organizational cultures.

The Mood Elevator has been enthusiastically embraced by hundreds of thousands of employees in Senn Delaney clients around the world. Many of them have expressed a desire to learn more about the Mood Elevator and to share it with friends and loved ones. The book is designed for them as well as for others who may only have the opportunity to learn about the Mood Elevator through this book.

While many ideas in the book are taught to clients in Senn Delaney sessions, many of the ideas and suggestions, including those about wellness, fitness and healthy living, come as a result of my own personal life journey and do not necessarily reflect the views of Senn Delaney in its work with organizations.

Senn Delaney's focus is on impacting the total organization, from the CEO's team to the frontline associates, through a comprehensive culture-shaping methodology. My focus in writing *Up the Mood Elevator* is simply to benefit individuals by bringing them ideas I have discovered through personal life experiences. My hope is that these ideas will help you ride the Mood Elevator in life with more grace and ease.

[GETTING TO KNOW THE MOOD ELEVATOR]

part one

THE MOOD ELEVATOR

grateful
wise, insightful
creative, innovative
resourceful
hopeful, optimistic
appreciative
patient, understanding
sense of humor
flexible, adaptive
curious, interested
impatient, frustrated
irritated, bothered
worried, anxious
defensive, insecure
judgmental, blaming
self-righteous
stressed, burned-out
angry, hostile
depressed

Chapter One

■■■■■■■■■■■■■■■■

[exploring the Mood Elevator]

You have probably already looked at the Mood Elevator on the opposite page. Most people are drawn to it magnetically. While it's something new, it's also something very familiar – it's the "human condition." It's our moment-to-moment experience of life. It encompasses a wide range of feelings; together, these emotions play a major role in defining the quality of our lives as well as our effectiveness.

We all move up and down the Mood Elevator every day. Wouldn't it be great if we knew the right button to push to move toward the top of our own personal Mood Elevator? And wouldn't it be helpful if there were ways to make our visits to the lower levels less intense and shorter in duration?

My purpose in writing *Up the Mood Elevator–Living Life at Your Best* is to share with you some profound principles, fascinating concepts and practical tools to improve your ride on your own Mood Elevator. That, in turn, will improve your experience of life, enhance your results, build better relationships and create more success with less stress.

Let's begin by exploring the Mood Elevator and how it relates to you and your life. Most of the levels are probably familiar to you; we have all visited them at one point or another in our lives. There are moments, hours or days when we are more lighthearted. We are in touch with things we are grateful for in our lives, we feel more secure, confident, creative and resourceful. We are not as easily bothered by people and situations, and are less apt to "sweat the small stuff." We are more curious than judgmental and have a better sense of humor. At times like these, you probably experience more ease and grace, are more in the flow of life and are better connected to wisdom or universal intelligence. At times like these, you are operating *"Up the Mood Elevator."*

But to be human means that we will spend some time "Down the Mood Elevator" as well. That means times when our life doesn't look or feel as good. Times we feel less secure and worry more. Times we are more easily irritated and bothered by people or circumstances and can be more judgmental, defensive and self-righteous. At other times we might feel just generally down, troubled or depressed. Our lower-level feelings can range from quite passive (low energy, worry or depression) to very intense and active (feeling self-righteous or angry).

The key to greater success, less stress and a richer life experience is to spend more time on the higher floors of the Mood Elevator and do less damage to ourselves and others when visiting the lower floors. That's important because we all visit the lower levels at times; being human means having both high moods and low moods.

I encourage you to familiarize yourself with the Mood Elevator because it will be your guide throughout this book.

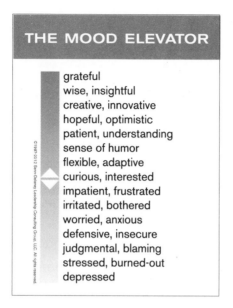

To begin, ask yourself the following questions:

- Which levels are most familiar to you as a part of your normal day-to-day experience of life?

- Which levels do you get stuck at when you are having a bad day?

- Which levels better define your temperament? In other words, how would most people describe you?

- Which levels would you like to have a lot more of in your life and which would you like to minimize?

- Which level is an early warning sign that your mood is dropping?

One of my personal signals that I'm headed south is when I notice I am becoming more impatient and more easily irritated or bothered. Something that someone says or does might get a reaction from me when I am in a lower state, yet be no big deal when I am in a healthier state.

I believe the Mood Elevator also catches people's attention because we all have a natural desire to have a better quality of life and to experience higher-level feelings more often. There is no question that living more of the time in the higher states of the Mood Elevator improves your life and the quality of your human experience. Who wouldn't want to feel more gratitude, love, humor and lightness? Who wouldn't benefit from more creativity, curiosity and resilience? Who wouldn't want to worry less, feel stress less and be irritated and bothered less often?

The Mood Elevators depicted in the book are hypothetical ones. They are based on my own experience and input from hundreds of groups and tens of thousands of people attending seminars designed or conducted by Senn Delaney, the world-wide culture-shaping firm I founded in 1978. The Mood Elevator illustrates what I perceive as the common human condition.

In reality, we each have our own unique Mood Elevator; you'll be asked to construct your own later in this book. In my personal Mood Elevator, one of the items at the top of my list is gratitude. It is a feeling I often have towards my wife, Bernadette, and our five children when I slow down, quiet my mind and am not preoccupied with the pressures of the day. It is a feeling that wells up in me when Logan, my 12-year-old, says, "I love you, Dad," or when I see a beautiful sunset with a multitude of colors filling the sky.

When I am on the upper levels of my Mood Elevator, I am also more likely to feel creative and resourceful. Ideas and answers come easier, and solutions to problems are more accessible.

I have grown to greatly value the feelings I experience when

I'm at my best. I believe my life is richer and my contribution to my family and friends, my church, and my chosen life's work is greater in direct proportion to my feelings of gratitude, love, creativity and curiosity. It's what drives me to want to write a book like this and share these thoughts with you.

In fact, writing is a great example of the value of the higher states. There are times when creative thoughts don't come at all, and other times when ideas and concepts come pouring out. When we are at our best and at the top of our game, it's almost as if we connect to a source of inspiration and ideas greater than ourselves – a form of universal intelligence and original thought.

The upper states of the Mood Elevator define those times when we have higher-quality thinking and function at our best. The lower states, when we are off our game, include feelings that come from lower-quality thinking. You can test this yourself by asking which level (higher or lower) is best for:

- Creating a trusting relationship?
- Discussing an issue with a loved one?
- Solving a complex problem?
- Making an important life decision?

The answer, of course, is "Up the Mood Elevator." The higher levels lead to more success with less stress, healthier relationships, better personal health and a better quality of life. It is a better place to parent from, a better place to lead from and a better place to build a career or family from.

Just imagine for a moment how different your life and relationships might be if you were to spend a lot more time on the upper floors of the Mood Elevator, and knew how to minimize the negative impact on yourself and others when you were on the lower levels.

While most people immediately relate to the concept of the Mood Elevator when they see it, very few have ever thought about their life experience in this way. That's probably because they assume it's "just the way life is," and that nothing can be done about the ups and downs.

It is true that to be human means we will all spend some time riding up and down the elevator. In fact, we all will visit most of the floors at one time or another. But have you known anyone who just moved in at Impatient, Worried, or Judgmental? Those are places we may periodically visit, but certainly not places we'd like to take up permanent residence. Your stay on those lower floors can be much briefer and the impact on you and others significantly lessened if you learn to use the suggestions on the following pages.

The purpose of this book is to provide you with some useful pointers on living life "Up the Mood Elevator." What you achieve in your personal and professional life can be profoundly impacted if you understand and practice the principles and pointers we are going to cover in *Up the Mood Elevator—Living Life at Your Best*. I've seen it happen to countless people, and I look forward to introducing you to these useful principles.

"I know of no more encouraging fact than the unquestionable ability of man to elevate his life by a conscious endeavor. To affect the quality of the day, that is the highest of arts."

– Henry David Thoreau

Chapter Two

■ ■ ■ ■ ■ ■ ■ ■ ■ ■ ■ ■ ■ ■ ■ ■

[where do moods come from?]

Many of the tips for riding the Mood Elevator require an understanding of where moods originate. That understanding alone can change your experience of life.

So where *do* moods come from? The answer may surprise you because it is not obvious nor is it what most people think.

Understanding where moods come from helps us deal with them. But gaining that understanding is not as simple as it seems. Some moods appear to come upon us out of the blue, much like a rainy day when it was sunny the day before. Some days life just doesn't look or feel as good. We get out of bed and have a little bit of an attitude. That must be where the old saying, "I got up on the wrong side of the bed" comes from.

If you ask most people where their low mood came from, they will probably tell you about something that happened to them or something someone said or did to them. Most people believe moods are caused by external circumstances. Something occurs that we don't like, or someone does something that pushes our buttons. This can take a variety of forms. A loved one makes a comment, or doesn't thank us when we really went out of our way to do something nice for them. The stock market goes down (again) or a boss or colleague at work blames us for something we didn't do. Maybe we step on the scale and don't like the number we see. Or we turn on our computer and notice too many emails piling up in our inbox that need a reply. Or our teenager brings home a date with multiple body piercings. Or we look at our to-do list and realize it's far too long. Or we are driving to work and get a ticket. Or we miss a stoplight, get caught in traffic or stuck in a line. I think you get the picture.

We encounter those challenges on a daily – if not hourly – basis, but that still doesn't explain where our moods come from.

Let me tell you a story about a friend named John, and let's see if you can figure out where John's moods originate.

As John leaves work, he appears quite upset. He has heard some disturbing news and decides to stop for a few minutes at a park on the way home to try to regain his composure. He sits down on a bench and recalls a conversation he had with a colleague just before leaving the office. He heard a rumor that the company was going to downsize. His co-worker said he thought it was likely to impact John's division.

John begins to think about all the possible consequences of being laid off and naturally, his spirits plummet. What if he can't find another job? Will he lose his home? A neighbor got laid off and lost his; it can happen that easily. Does it mean his kids won't be able to go to college? Can his ego handle being fired and the repercussions of what others will think? How will he tell his wife, since he knows how much she worries? John proceeds to move systematically down the Mood Elevator from anxious to worried to downright depressed.

He then thinks downsizing is a heartless thing for the company to do. How had they gotten themselves into this position? Was the decision made just to benefit the bosses at the top? That moves John to initially feel judgment; then resentment, anger and some self-righteousness follow as he thinks about all the years he's put in and all the hard work he's done to make it a great company. By now he has toured the entire bottom half of the Mood Elevator – and then some.

But wait, rumors like this have circled around before and have never proven to be true. His co-worker is a known rumor mill, and this isn't the first time the same colleague has talked about things that have never come to pass. John heaves a sigh of relief and says to himself, "It's probably not true at all!" He moves back up the Mood Elevator to neutral and a bit curious.

From this higher vantage point, he notices his thoughts going in a different direction. He says to himself, "You know, for some time now I've been thinking of moving on to a job that suits me better, and I haven't had the courage to do it. Maybe if this layoff does happen, I'll have to leave my comfortable job, take a severance package and I might find something a whole lot more fulfilling. I've had other friends who have left and they never looked back."

Even if only a rumor, John was grateful that it had given him a wake-up call and made him think more about his future and what was really important. His job was no longer stimulating and he didn't feel it made full use of his abilities and potential.

He thought about the kinds of things he would love to do, and he became quite inspired.

John then looked up and saw children playing in the park. It put him in touch with the fact that the most important thing to him was his family: his wife, son and daughter and the loving relationship they have. That moved him up to gratitude at the top of the Mood Elevator as he prepared to go home and share some quality time with his family.

So what *did* cause John's wild fluctuations in moods as he sat in the park? Right. It was his *thinking*! Each level on the Mood Elevator John visited was accompanied by a thought. **So it's our thinking that creates our moods.**

> "Man is made or unmade by himself. As the lord of his own thoughts, he holds the key to every situation."
>
> – James Allen, *As a Man Thinketh*

There may be events that trigger our thoughts but it's important to remember that we are the thinker. We create our own moods out of what happens to us in life.

We can see how it works by going back to some of the earlier illustrations of things that happen in our life. With the speeding ticket, our thinking could have ranged from beating ourselves up for not paying attention to being angry with the officer for giving us a ticket when others going the same speed weren't cited. Or, we could have been relaxed about it and just noted it was a good (but expensive) reminder to pay more attention while driving.

When someone blamed us for something at work, we could have felt anger toward them – or we could have just written it off to the fact that they might be having a bad day. And we might have looked for the grain of truth in what they said to see what we could learn.

In each case, wherever our thinking went, that's where our mood went. It's as if we are each making a movie in our heads. Not only have we been given the power of thought, but also the consciousness or related feelings to take whatever our thinking is and make it real. It's as if we have our own Hollywood special effects department to go along with our thoughts.

It follows, then, that:

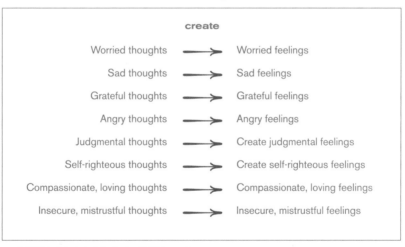

create

Worried thoughts	⟶	Worried feelings
Sad thoughts	⟶	Sad feelings
Grateful thoughts	⟶	Grateful feelings
Angry thoughts	⟶	Angry feelings
Judgmental thoughts	⟶	Create judgmental feelings
Self-righteous thoughts	⟶	Create self-righteous feelings
Compassionate, loving thoughts	⟶	Compassionate, loving feelings
Insecure, mistrustful thoughts	⟶	Insecure, mistrustful feelings

It does appear on the surface that our moods come from the outside – usually from two sources. The first is the conditions or circumstances of our life. The second is what other people do or say. We are worried because we are facing some challenges. We are irritated or bothered because someone did or said something we didn't like. We're happy because our team won, we got the raise, or our children brought home a good report card. It's the way life appears to us – because people and events create our feelings and experience.

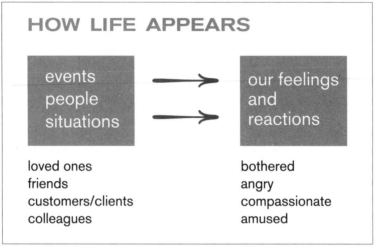

HOW LIFE APPEARS

| events people situations | → → | our feelings and reactions |

loved ones
friends
customers/clients
colleagues

bothered
angry
compassionate
amused

But there's still more to it than that. It's not the circumstances of our life; as in John's story about the rumored layoffs, it's what we make of the circumstances. As a great writer once said:

"There is nothing either good or bad but thinking makes it so."

– William Shakespeare

The variable between the event and our reaction is our thinking or "what we make of it."

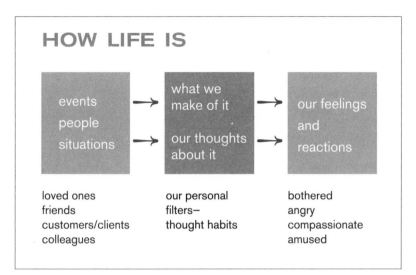

HOW LIFE IS

events people situations	what we make of it · our thoughts about it	our feelings and reactions
loved ones friends customers/clients colleagues	our personal filters– thought habits	bothered angry compassionate amused

When we at Senn Delaney were considering being acquired by a large organization a number of years ago, half the employees were excited about the added opportunities it would bring through increased leads, broader capabilities and added investments that could help us grow faster. The other half were considering updating their resumes and looking elsewhere because they were sure we'd lose the unique culture we had if we were acquired. It was the same event but two totally different interpretations. Each group was creating a story about the future and then reacting to that story.

We see it in everyday life. We end a challenging day tired, a bit overwhelmed by what we have to face tomorrow and a bit discouraged by what we didn't accomplish today. We get a good night's sleep, get up and take a walk or run and miraculously, life looks fine. We start the new day more hopeful and optimistic. Nothing in our circumstances has changed. The only thing that's changed is our thinking about it – the story in our head.

One day a child or loved one does something and it seems cute. They do the same thing the next day and it's irritating. Nothing has changed except the way we view it.

I have five children that range in age from 12 to 47. The youngest, Logan, was born when I was past retirement age for most people. Because Kendra, our next oldest child, is nine years older and away at college, Logan is almost like an only child. Therefore, I often end up being Logan's playmate in sports, video games or surfing.

Most weekends when he says, "Let's play, Dad!" I say to myself what a lucky man I am and I think about all the positive things Logan has brought into my life. He sees the world through the eyes of a child with all the freshness and curiosity that brings. He helps keep me young and flexible; he helps me learn and grow; and he has increased my commitment to health and fitness so I can be here for him and keep up with him.

On an occasional Saturday or Sunday when I'd rather sleep in, relax or recharge, and he jumps on me and says the exact same thing he always says: "Let's play, Dad!" I think, "That was a dumb thing to add to the family so late in life. You don't get to sleep in or just read the book or watch that favorite TV program. Why in the world did you agree to another child?"

It's the same Logan jumping on me in the early morning. It's my thinking and what I make of it that makes the difference. Life is largely what we make of it through our thinking.

Fortunately, my thoughts about Logan are overwhelmingly about the love he gives, the joy he brings and the person he is helping me to become. That brings me deep feelings of love, inspiration and gratitude.

Think of times when you are down on the Mood Elevator. Where does your thinking go? While it's true that events can trigger our thinking, it's our thinking that creates our feelings or mood. It's that Hollywood special effects department again – built into us to bring every thought alive.

Our thinking has a powerful effect on us physically as well as mentally. Worrying about something creates the same physical effects as if what you are worrying about actually happened. Worry thoughts can raise your blood pressure, increase your heart rate and create other physical manifestations even though what we are worrying about hasn't actually occurred and probably won't – or won't be as bad as we think.

The Movie in Our Mind

We once had a consultant named Deborah who joined us from a senior position at Continental Airlines headquarters in Houston. Consultants at Senn Delaney can live wherever they choose since they fly to most engagements. Deb elected to stay in Houston. Shortly after she joined us and began her training, I had a sales call with a CEO of a major utility company in Houston. I decided to invite Deb to join me since it was in her home town. I thought it could give her a chance to hear how we talked about Senn Delaney to a prospective client and it might create some work for her in Houston. Little did I know what that innocent invitation would do to Deb's thinking.

As she described it later, it went something like this: "A sales call with the chairman of my new company? What if I perform badly? I'm just getting to know Senn Delaney; what will I say? I'm not a sales person, I joined to do culture-shaping consulting – that's what I know, not selling. What if I embarrass us and we lose the sale? I could get fired. I took a risk leaving my long-time employer and I can't go back now. That would look awful on my resume. What if I can't get another job? My oldest child won't be able to start college like he is planning on, and I could lose the house."

As we laughed about it later, she said that when her imagination temporarily ran away on her, she pictured herself homeless, living in a cardboard box under the freeway. It turned out quite differently. It was a very successful meeting. Deb attended the same church as the CEO and they had mutual friends. We got the culture-shaping engagement with the CEO and as a part of a larger team, Deb got some work in Houston and didn't have to travel for it.

We all go through life interpreting each and every thing others do, each and every event and projecting our own story about what it means. We can take the same event and create a happy ending or a disastrous one, all in our minds, before anything ever happens.

Have you ever gotten really mad at someone for something – and then found out they didn't do it? Have you ever been really sure that something bad would happen and it didn't? We all have. In each case we had to live through it as if it actually did happen unless we understood the power of thought.

Understanding the power of thought and the role it plays in our feelings gives us the same power as when we go to see a movie. You sit in the theater all caught up in the action, drama or suspense in a horror movie. The music is playing. You may be having physical sensations including fear or anxiety, but on some level you know it's just a movie. You know you can go get popcorn if it gets too scary and that you're going to be able to walk out at the end – because you know it's not real. If we could treat some of our own "mental" movies that way, our thinking would have a lot less power over us. Our thoughts and imagination can feel like it's the real thing. Knowing we are the thinker and that our thoughts are creating our feelings gives us just a little distance from them even if we can't let them go completely.

Our Thinking and Dreams

Another interesting analogy is dreams – especially nightmares. If you've ever awakened right after having one, you remember how real it feels. Maybe you were being chased or threatened, or you couldn't find something of importance or the place you desperately needed to be. You were probably glad you woke up with the realization "that was just a bad dream." It wasn't real. It occurred only in our minds and our thinking made it so. But it sure feels as if it was real.

The Underlying Principles

The underlying principles needed to understand our moods and how we can operate at our best are fairly simple. Learning how to use them to spend more time up the Mood Elevator takes a deeper understanding.

The simple underlying principles we will be exploring to gain this understanding include the following:

- We are born with access to a naturally healthy state of mind. Our default setting is to be "Up the Mood Elevator." That's our home base – and it's only a thought away.

- We are born with the power of thought and it is through thought that we experience life and ride up and down the Mood Elevator.

- The way we experience life is through our feelings or moods. Our feelings bring our thoughts to life through all the emotions and sensations we experience – from joy right on down to depression.

How is this understanding helpful? Understanding that our thinking creates our reality helps us spend less time blaming our feelings on events and others.

Just knowing that it's our thoughts – and we are the thinker – gives us a bit more control over our lives. Knowing that it's our thinking gives us just a little bit of distance. In this way, we can be less gripped by worry, fear and anxiety and less certain in our judgments of other people and other things.

> "We are formed and molded by our thoughts. Those whose minds are shaped by selfless thoughts give joy when they speak or act. Joy follows them like a shadow that never leaves them."
>
> – Buddha

Chapter Three

■■■■■■■■■■■■■■■■■

[the payoff: success with less stress]

The payoff for gaining an understanding of the role of thought goes far beyond a better moment-to-moment experience of life. It can help you have a more successful career, more fulfilling job, more loving marriage and healthier relationships. It can create more success with less stress in your life.

That's because when we are at our best and up the Mood Elevator, we have what could be called *higher-quality thinking.* Our thoughts are clearer. We are better focused. Our thinking is more organized, our thoughts more flowing. At times like this, we may feel like we are "in the zone." Mihaly Csikszentmihalyi, former chairman of the Department of Psychology at the University of Chicago, has studied this phenomenon. He wrote about it in the book *Flow: The Psychology of Optimal Experience.* Csikszentmihalyi found that there are "flow times" that all people have when they are absorbed and in tune with what they are doing. During these flow times, people have exceptionally clear, creative and resourceful thinking, as well as appropriate answers to whatever situation they are dealing with. It seems to come to them naturally and effortlessly.

These don't need to be exceptional times. While no one is

always in the zone, a form of "flow state" can become a way of life.

In contrast to being in flow, have you ever been late getting somewhere, felt really rushed, frustrated, bothered or extremely impatient, with nothing going quite right? Notice what your thinking is like in these situations. Mine is very scattered and unfocused. I may rush out of the house late for a meeting and realize I forgot something important, like the car keys or my GPS. In my haste, I find it harder than normal to do even the smallest thing right. The car key doesn't fit in the ignition as easily or effortlessly as when I am calm. My thoughts race. Solutions aren't as forthcoming. The same can happen if I get overly excited, emotional or intense.

In times like that we are down the Mood Elevator and we have what could be called *lower-quality thinking*. Thoughts aren't as clear and answers aren't as obvious. When our thoughts turn to worry or insecurity, they are often circular – going around and around. Our thinking is busy and more cluttered. During times like these, we don't hear others as well. We aren't as tuned in to other people, what is on their mind or the impact we are having on them.

On the other hand, have you ever been wrestling with an issue, then let it go and then, when you're feeling less tense (perhaps while doing something else), a creative solution occurs to you? With your quieter mind, you actually slip into higher-quality thinking. We often do that when we relax. In fact, one study showed that the place most people report having the most new or creative ideas is while taking a shower. Strange as that may sound, the world is blocked out when we're showering, so our mind quiets down and answers to things we may have been thinking about suddenly appear.

When we are at our best and have higher-quality thinking, we have full access to the capabilities of our mind. The chart below illustrates the varied capabilities of the mind, ranging from the more basic uses (such as memory and processing) right on up to the highest levels of insight and wisdom. When we are in the higher states of the Mood Elevator, we have access simultaneously to all of these levels.

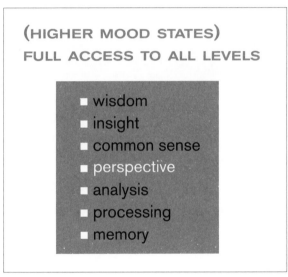

(HIGHER MOOD STATES)
FULL ACCESS TO ALL LEVELS

■ wisdom
■ insight
■ common sense
■ perspective
■ analysis
■ processing
■ memory

When we drop down the Mood Elevator and get trapped in our own lower-quality thinking, we can still tap in to our memory, but it's much more filtered – and less of it is available to us. We can still process information and data, but we lose access to common sense, wisdom and intuition.

When we are out of touch with ourselves and not tuned in to others, we also say and do things we wouldn't normally do; we neglect to "keep our wits about us" (as Rudyard Kipling would say). This loss of our higher functioning can be seen in the chart below.

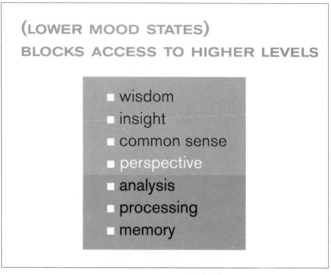

It is no accident that the dividing line between higher- and lower-quality thinking is **perspective**. As long as we are able to keep people, events and life itself in perspective, we have our bearings. When we lose perspective, we lose access to our higher-quality thinking.

Emotional Intelligence

There is a scientific explanation for why people who are more conscious of their moment-to-moment feelings do better in life, are more successful and more fulfilled. It is because they have higher Emotional Intelligence (EQ).

Daniel Goleman, the author of *Emotional Intelligence: Why It Can Matter More Than IQ*, and *Primal Leadership: Realizing the Power of Emotional Intelligence*, has probably done more than anyone else to explain the benefits of EQ and the difference between what we normally call intelligence or Intellectual Quotient (IQ) and the concept behind EQ.

Viewed from the standpoint of the Mood Elevator, people with EQ have a higher moment-to-moment awareness of where they are on the Mood Elevator and the impact they are having on others. They do and say what comes naturally when in a higher mood state and are cautious or don't do or say what's on their mind when in a lower mood state.

A study that Goleman cites is one in which Harvard graduates from classes in the 1940s were followed into middle age to see who would be more successful. Surprisingly, those with the highest test scores (IQ) did not fare as well as their lower-scoring peers. Significant differences could be found in salary, professional status, life satisfaction, happiness, friendships and family. It seemed that success in life and career is less tied to intellect than it is to emotional awareness and control.

When it comes to life success and satisfaction, EQ trumps IQ. The good news is that EQ can be learned, whereas IQ is fairly static.

Goleman tells the fable of a belligerent samurai who challenges his Zen master to explain the concept of heaven and hell. The monk replied in a belittling way, "You're nothing but a bully – I can't waste my time on someone like you."

Feeling his honor attacked, the samurai flew into a rage, pulled out his sword and yelled, "I could kill you for your impertinence." The monk simply replied, "And there is your hell." Stunned by the comment, the samurai fell to his knees and begged forgiveness for his lack of wisdom. The monk replied, "And that is heaven."

Cultivating an awareness of where you are on the Mood Elevator, especially during times when you are below the level of Curious, is demonstrating true EQ. Learning how to shift your mental state (and during times when you are unable to, learning how to do less damage), is a key to emotional intelligence and more success with less stress in life.

The samurai was facing one of the most challenging emotions people have to address: anger or rage. In her research, Dianne M. Tice, PhD, professor of psychology at Florida State University, found that anger is the mood people have the most difficulty controlling. That's partly because it's the most seductive: We feel the most self-righteous when we are in its grip. We have this conversation in our head that is very convincing in terms of why our intense feelings are justified. The justification is the situation we face or the person causing our feelings, and we think we have every right to feel and act the way we do. Unlike sadness, which is more of a low, passive feeling, anger can be energizing, even exhilarating, and we can get swept up in it. Anger also comes with a loud inner monologue egging us on.

Loss of Emotional Intelligence When Stressed

There is a scientific explanation for why we can lose our EQ in stressful situations. Amy F. T. Arnsten, PhD, professor of neurobiology at Yale University School of Medicine, has found that stressful situations cause the higher-reasoning centers in our brain to shut down, while at the same time allowing the more primal areas of our brain to take over.

As adrenaline is released during high-stress moments, it inhibits the prefrontal cortex, where higher reasoning takes place. Adrenaline then stimulates the amygdala (aka "lizard brain"), which is where our "fight or flight" reaction kicks in as we cope with our conditioned fear and loss of control reflexes.

This result is what Arnsten calls "the biology of feeling frazzled," a fascinating mix of extreme and narrow focus and loss of concentration. Our ability to intake information (and clues) diminishes and all our senses are focused in a single direction. Our intensity increases and choices seem obvious, but our thinking is unreliable and our reactions usually inappropriate.

At the extreme end of the spectrum, our social impairment and EQ reaches the level of mind-blindness – in other words, a complete and utter lack of insight and empathy. Even at moderate levels we start to lose touch with the complexity of social situations. We begin to act in short-term, self-protective ways that come across as selfish, defensive and self-centered. In short, when it matters most, we're often at our worst.

In contrast, the answer to why people with higher EQs do well in life can be seen by taking a look at the Mood Elevator and the benefits of higher-quality thinking. When we are in the higher mood states, we are more resourceful, more creative and more innovative. We are more patient, understanding and compassionate. Is it any wonder, then, that we deal with life issues better when we have a larger tool kit?

We deal better because we are more observant when we are up the Mood Elevator. We listen better, we see more and are more open to possibilities. As a result, people with higher EQ have better support systems, better networks and better relationships. They have more resources at their disposal.

When we are down the Mood Elevator, we are trapped in our own filters. We have what is called "selective perception." We don't hear as well, see as well, or take in all the appropriate information. An example of selective perception is when we get stuck in a rigid point of view – what might be called a fixed mindset. Once we have decided something is a certain away, we can only see things that support that position and become blind to other ways of viewing it. As a result, we have fewer options and fewer choices. We also become harder to deal with.

One of the few television programs I watch is *The Mentalist*. This show is a great example of EQ in action. The central character, Patrick Jane (played by Simon Baker), is a consultant for the fictional California Bureau of Investigation. *The Mentalist* is a graphic and often amusing example of someone who can take in more, notice more and think outside the box. People are always referring to Patrick as a psychic – and he replies that there is no such thing. He is just extremely observant. He sees subtle things in crime scenes no one else sees. He comes to amazingly accurate conclusions about people quickly, through keen observation. He can tell when people are lying through their body language, eye movement, pulse rate and other clues that others can't detect. He takes in more (and connects the dots better) than those around him. He is generally calm, relaxed, and lighthearted and seems to do what he does with ease and grace.

I have always had a belief that people who could see and

know what others don't know have highly accurate intuition. But they are, in fact, just people who are better tuned in to their environment and better able to read subtle signals most of us don't notice. I believe we all have this capability. Our minds are just too busy and cluttered to take advantage of it. Self-awareness – coupled with awareness of those around us – is part of the answer to high emotional intelligence; so is living life at our best and having more success with less stress.

> "I think we all have a little voice inside us that will guide us... if we shut out all the noise and clutter from our lives and listen to that voice, it will tell us the right thing to do."
>
> – Christopher Reeve

I've noticed that I move into the flow state when I'm more ego-less, less self-centered and more purpose driven. It happens to me most when I am coaching, facilitating a seminar about these concepts, or explaining to a prospective client the benefits of having a more purposeful, thriving culture. When I'm in the flow state, my mind is clear. I'm not self-conscious. I just am. I listen for understanding with a quieter mind. I can notice when something I say makes sense to the listener and when it doesn't – I know when they are with me and when they are drifting away.

But as soon as I start worrying about how I am doing, how I look or if I'll be successful, it's like the bubble bursts. I am no longer in that state. My feelings shift from a more effortless flow to a busier mind and a feeling that is less comfortable. That's a signal that I've dropped down the Mood Elevator into Insecure or one of the other lower states.

Mental Traction

Things work out better for those who can maintain their bearings in spite of circumstances. People who maintain higher EQ fare better in relationships, discussions, debates and confrontations.

People who lose their cool are at a distinct disadvantage. I know that if I can keep my bearings in spite of inappropriate behavior by someone I am dealing with, I'll come out ahead. It is when I lose my mental traction that I am at a disadvantage.

I carry a mental image of this state that has served me well. Many years ago, I saw an illusionist's act at Universal Studios. The illusionist asked three of the strongest-looking guys in the audience to come up on stage, take off their shoes and stand in a spot he designated.

Next, the illusionist asked a petite woman to join them on stage and stand on another designated spot about 10 feet away from the men. He then gave the men one end of a rope and the woman the other end, and asked them to have a "tug of war." To everyone's amazement, the woman began to pull the three large men toward her across the floor.

It turns out that the guys were asked to stand on a spot that had been made extremely slippery, and they couldn't get any traction in their stocking feet. In contrast, the woman was placed on a special rubber pad with lots of traction so it didn't take much to move the men.

When we drop down the Mood Elevator, especially when we don't adjust for it, we lose our mental traction. We can't think as clearly, communicate as well or react as quickly.

Remember the tug-of-war image the next time you are dealing with a difficult person. Then take a deep breath, bring to mind the fact that they are just driven by their own thinking and try not to take what they are saying personally. Do whatever you need to do to keep your mental traction. You'll get a far better outcome.

Original Thought

Another reason that we do better in the higher mood states is that we have access to what could be called "original thought." Most of what goes on in our thinking is not new or creative. We are usually just reprocessing what's already in our memory bank or sorting new input into categories based on something we already know or have previously experienced. Ever notice that when you mention children, the people you are talking to will tell you about theirs? Or you say vacation, and they will tell you about their favorite one? That's because nothing new has entered the system.

Explaining what we already know and sorting new information into our own categories is a practical use of the capacity of the mind. However, only a limited amount of thinking can be categorized as original thought – ideas that just occur to us out of the blue. They are the ones that have new meaning or significance and are not already a part of our experience. These come from the highest levels: The insight and wisdom levels in the mind. Some people would say they even come from beyond our experience – from universal intelligence.

Original thought is the source of breakthroughs and inventions, new solutions to old problems and the answers to new ways of seeing and doing things we haven't done before. While riding in his 1988 Chevy Blazer on 4th of July in 1994 a young engineer named Jeff Bezos had just such a new thought. He was able to envision the then fledgling internet as a distribution system for products to the masses. He sketched out a business plan for an internet shopping business beginning with books. He laid the groundwork for a retail revolution and called it Amazon after the river with its thousands of branches and tributaries.

We all know practical, real-world examples of this phenomenon. We may be struggling with a project or situation or person, and seeing very few options because our energy is down and we are tired or dispirited. Then we get a good night's sleep, take a break, or have the weekend off and all of a sudden a range of possibilities appear before us. The more you learn ways to cultivate this phenomenon in your life, the more success and less stress you'll experience in your life and the higher the EQ you'll have.

In contrast, when we are in the lower mood states, we lose our perspective. The options available to us narrow and our thinking is much more restricted and purely memory based. We are more inclined to cling to the old than to visualize the possibilities of the new. We are less flexible, less resilient, less open minded. We tend to say and do more things that are inappropriate and don't fit the situation. (We all have examples of things we've said and done in a low mood that we wish we hadn't.)

I once heard a story that is probably more of a modern parable, but it really drives home the point of EQ and IQ. It is a story about a single-engine airplane that is flying over very rough terrain when the engine goes out. There is no place to land and the plane is certainly going to crash. The only option is to bail out, but there is a problem. There are four people on the airplane but only three parachutes. The four people on board are the Secretary General of the United Nations, the smartest man in the world, a priest and an Eagle Scout.

The Secretary General immediately jumps up and says, *"I owe myself to the world and to humanity."* He grabs a chute and out he goes. Next up jumps the smartest man in the world. He says, *"I owe my mind to posterity,"* and out he goes.

There sits the priest and the Eagle Scout. The priest says to the scout, *"My son, I've lived a long and full life."* The scout merely replies, *"Don't worry about it Father, we each still have a chute – the smartest man in the world just grabbed my back-pack and he's on his way down with that now."*

Having knowledge, skills or even a high level of intelligence does not necessarily equip us to live the most successful or ful-filling life. This is especially true in stressful situations. It's when we may need it most that we aren't always able to see what we must in order to make the right choices in life.

My hope is that this book and the Mood Elevator will give you the tools, the understanding and the ability to see what you need to see in order to live your life with more awareness, more original thought, more success and greater fulfillment.

Chapter Four

■ ■ ■ ■ ■ ■ ■ ■ ■ ■ ■ ■ ■ ■ ■ ■

[the payoff in the performance of organizations]

I t's no accident that many of Senn Delaney's clients who bring concepts like the Mood Elevator and role of thought to life in their organizations can be found on the industry lists of *Fortune's* "Most Admired" companies. Many also have J.D. Power awards for customer service and rank high on Gallup employee engagement scores.

A fundamental belief in our culture-shaping work is that we don't have to *teach* our clients anything; we just have to give them insights and practical ways to reconnect to the best of who they already are. That happens naturally for people and organizations when they are up the Mood Elevator. We simply call it operating "At Our Best." When leaders and teams are at their best, their innately healthy behaviors come to life and organizations flourish.

One of my deeply held beliefs, and the premise of this book, is that we all come into this world with what could be called innate health – an inborn set of values or behaviors. Our natural state is to be loving, creative, trusting, forgiving, curious, happy and desirous of warm, close relationships with others.

It's easy to see this state in very young children. To them, life is a wonder. They are spontaneous and they live in the moment. They get over things easily and don't hold grudges. They are naturally up the Mood Elevator much of the time – and when they go down the elevator, they don't stay there for long periods like adults can do. In large part that's because children hold their thinking more lightly and haven't decided on how things are supposed to be yet.

However, as we grow up in our family of origin and have experiences in life, we develop "thought habits" or beliefs that can mask or obscure that innate health. We feel hurt by someone and become more guarded or defensive. We are criticized for a mistake and learn to make excuses and become less accountable. We play sports and learn there is usually a winner and a loser, so we adopt a self-centered "win-lose" mindset. We are judged for "being ourselves" so we develop an alter ego that is not authentic. Unfortunately, in a down mood our thought habits can drive us and we lose that healthy child-like gift we had.

Songwriters Eric Bazilian and Rob Hyman capture this phenomenon very poetically in the lyrics of a song they wrote called:

Where Do the Children Go?

Where do the children go between the bright light and the darkest day? Where do the children go, and who is the deadly piper that leads them away?

Many of the learned habits that people develop growing up show up as dysfunctions in organizations they become a part of. Trust issues arise. Inauthentic politics thrive. Departments and functions blame one another. Win-lose battles play out every day.

When Senn Delaney performs our cultural diagnostics with a new client one of the scores on our Corporate Culture Profile™ most often found in the "Red" (or seriously dysfunctional) zone is "Stress and Burnout." That is not surprising. These days most organizations operate with fewer people doing more work at a faster pace than ever before – often in less than healthy corporate cultures. The concepts in this book consistently move our clients out of the "Red" zone and toward a "Healthy Fast Paced" rating. It is empowering for our clients to learn that they have access to the healthy thinking, feelings and behaviors that can elude them when their thinking is down the Mood Elevator. Clients learn that healthy organizational behaviors are only a thought away – and they learn how to access them.

I discovered a useful metaphor about our innate health when I was fishing with my son Logan. We were using a "bobber," a plastic ball that floats on the water's surface with the line and bait dangling beneath it. It's called a bobber because you can see it move when the fish starts to nibble on the bait. The fish periodically pulls the bobber under the water but the bobber's natural state is to bob back up to the surface – just as our natural state is to be up the Mood Elevator. Thoughts of worry, judgment and insecurity are like the fish – and they can sometimes nibble at us and pull us under temporarily. But when we can quiet our minds and let go of those thoughts, our natural health pops back up.

Universal Life Effectiveness Principles: The Essential Values

Senn Delaney's work in organizations generally begins with the senior teams. We help them define a set of values that become the rules of the road for behavior within their organization. This set of values defines the kind of culture they want.

We do this as one part of an overall culture-shaping plan through work with the CEO's team in an off-site retreat. By the end of the two- or three-day session, most people are really operating at their best and the group is at the top of the Mood Elevator. While the team is in that healthy state, we ask how they want to be with one another – and what values they want for their organization. They spontaneously create a list that paints a picture of a healthy, high-performing team and organization.

A few years ago, after having done this with hundreds of groups, we began to notice that the lists the groups spontaneously made were very similar. We concluded that when we get any group in a really healthy place – up the Mood Elevator – they identify what we now call "The Essential Value Set."

We've found that the most successful individuals, teams and organizations live these essential values better than others who are less successful and fulfilled in their lives. The list contains all the behaviors that are natural for people when they are in the higher states of the Mood Elevator and very difficult to exhibit for people when they are in the lower states.

The list includes the following:

- a foundation of a positive, optimistic spirit with respect, trust, recognition and caring and a healthy state of mind vs. pessimism, cynicism and mistrust

- personal accountability and a desire for excellence vs. blaming and excuses

- mutually supportive relationships and teamwork for the greater good vs. selfishness, turf issues and "we/ they" politics

- curiosity and an open, learning mindset supported by encouragement to take risks and innovate vs. judgment and resistance to new ideas

- integrity and authenticity vs. pretenses and a lack of transparency

- purpose – including a connection to the organization's noble cause or reason for existence, and a desire to focus on that greater good vs. self-interest

These principles can be easily translated to our overall lives and relationships outside of work as well. When we are "At Our Best" (in the flow and up the Mood Elevator), we are naturally more positive, hopeful and optimistic. We are committed to something bigger than ourselves, be it family, a higher power or the welfare of others. We are more resourceful and accountable vs. being victims. We are more curious than judgmental and more authentic and open.

We have found these principles to be consistent in our work in more than 40 countries around the world and in groups ranging from Fortune 500 and Global 1000 senior teams to university president's teams and Kindergarten through 8th graders and their teachers. We believe these are universal principles of life effectiveness for individuals as well as organizations.

It is fascinating to see how these principles play out in organizations. One example is Limited Brands – the parent company of Bath & Body Works and the mega-brand Victoria's Secret. The "Essential Values" show up at Limited Brands as *The Limited Way* – their aspirational cultural definition. While many business organizations have come under fire for unethical behaviors, Les Wexner, Limited Brands founder and CEO often says it is not just about winning, "It matters how you play the game."

Limited Brands is an exceptional organization in many ways. They were named by *Fortune* magazine as the Most Admired Specialty Retailer in America last year. Their same store sales gains topped those of competitors. The Center for Effective Organizations at University of Southern California (USC) has recognized them as one of the most agile companies in America.

In a global associate opinion survey including many of the world's best companies, Limited Brands was "First in the World" in a number of categories including:

- Decisions and actions reflect customer care

- I feel valued as an associate

- I have the opportunity to develop the skills I need to be successful in the future

- It is easy for people of diverse backgrounds to fit in – and be accepted

In acknowledging these achievements Les said, "It is our Thinking driving our Behaviors and our Results."

You'll hear concepts like the Mood Elevator, the Role of Thought and Shadow of the Leader in Limited Brands' meetings and leaders' presentations, and you'll find an understanding of the Mood Elevator and the need to lift the spirits and self-esteem of customers is well understood in the more than 1,000 Victoria's Secret stores around the world.

David Novak CEO of YUM! Brands with 36,000 KFC, Pizza Hut and Taco Bell restaurants around the world has effectively used the Mood Elevator as a tool to shape their culture and drive the employee and customer experience and results. David was named CEO of the Year for his accomplishments. YUM! Brands is one of a handful of large global companies that holds the distinction of delivering a decade of 10% plus earnings growth.

David took over when the brand was not doing that well and focused on creating a "recognition" culture with a positive spirit. He has taken that around the world and written a best selling book about it called *Taking People with You*. David included a section on the Mood Elevator in his book. In a CEO Show interview he talked about the obligation of leaders and the shadow they cast. He said, "The worst thing you can do is go to work every day and not have a positive attitude. You've got to at least move yourself up the Mood Elevator and get in the 'curious and interested' level to be an effective leader."

General Josue "Joe" Robles is CEO of USAA, the military insurance and financial services company. A much decorated military officer, he was named "Innovator of the Year" by American Banker Magazine. USAA has repeatedly been number one of all companies in America in surveys on customer service and customer loyalty. Joe and the USAA organization are driven by a noble mission of serving those who serve us and by a healthy set of values. Joe sees the Mood Elevator as a tool to bring out the best in people and in teams. As he says "The concept has been invaluable in all walks of life for people at USAA. It helps us work better together as business colleagues, but has equal benefit in personal relationships."

Unfortunately, organizations and individuals have a tendency to neglect what they consider the "soft" stuff, like personal awareness for individuals and culture for organizations. But it's that soft stuff that determines success in life and in organizations, and that's a big payoff.

Chapter Five

■■■■■■■■■■■■■■■■

[look to your feelings as your guide]

nce you conclude there is value in learning to better ride the Mood Elevator – how do we do it? The first and most important clue is to **"Look to Your Feelings as Your Guide."**

It may be hard to accept, but to a large degree we create our own feelings. Or, more precisely, our *thoughts* create our feelings. That's surprising, isn't it? Someone says something that "hurts your feelings," and you become sad. Another driver cuts in front of you on the freeway, and you are very upset – possibly even angry – even though you have probably inadvertently cut off some other driver sometime in your life. But in that moment when you have been cut off, they are that inconsiderate, irresponsible driver.

Once we understand that our thinking creates our moods, we still have a challenge. Here is the problem: Our thinking is largely invisible to us, and we can generally justify it no matter how unreasonable it may be. Therefore, our thinking does not serve as a very trustworthy guide to let us know how we are doing.

But there is good news. Fortunately, as human beings we were endowed with not only the power of thought through which to experience the world, but with the power of feelings as well. Each thought creates a feeling. And while the thought may be invisible, the feeling is detectable – and an important signal. The Mood Elevator is really just a "feelings barometer." So if you want to know how you are doing, the answer is: **Look to your feelings as your guide.**

In this way, you have clues to the reliability of your thinking and the impact it is having, not only on you but on those around you.

The Human Dashboard

The dashboard on a car provides an interesting analogy. Most of us drive cars. They are equipped with all kinds of gauges and warning systems to let us know how things are going. Most of these are on the dashboard. The Mood Elevator is much like a human dashboard in that it can let us know how things are going for us. Just like when we have a red light indicator to tell us if the car is overheating, we have that feeling called anger. Our gas gauge lets us know when we are low on fuel, but if we pay attention we can tell when our energy is way down and we are out of gas. If we use a navigational system like a GPS, the voice says "recalculating" when we make a wrong turn. If you learn to pay attention to your feelings, they, too, can be your guide and help you to "recalculate."

Part of this book was written using digital dictating equipment, because when I am in the flow I think faster than I can type. While working on this chapter, I was driving on the highway near our summer home in northern Wisconsin with a hands-free voice recorder. I was driving an older car, and it was a very hot day. I first stopped to get fuel because the fuel gauge started blinking, indicating I was running low on gas.

Because it was a very hot day, the main thing I kept my eye on, as you might guess, was the temperature gauge because of my fear of the old car overheating. Whenever the temperature gauge started to creep up too high, I would turn off the air conditioning to take that load off the small engine. Sure enough, the needle would move back down.

Are there times you are emotionally overheating or running low on energy and finding yourself slipping down the Mood Elevator into a more pessimistic state? Times you aren't sure you can handle all the things in front of you? Times you are in a less hopeful state and feeling a bit depressed?

If you got a good night's sleep or took a real weekend break and your energy (or "fuel") came back up again, my guess is the world would have looked different and better. The question is: How well did you read that signal? Was it soon enough, and did you know what to do to re-energize yourself? Do you know when and how to fill your tank?

Much like a car overheating, have there been times when you became emotionally overheated and might have been self-righteous or even angry? Once again, did you catch that soon enough? Did you know what to do to take some of the load off your emotional engine, so you could come back to your natural and healthier state?

That's the value in the Mood Elevator. It acts like a human dashboard to let us know how we are doing. If you can learn to notice your lower state feelings and use that to trigger some of the pointers in this book, you can live your life more often up the Mood Elevator – and at your best.

Dealing with Familiar Feelings

We all have what could be called "old familiar feelings." The lower levels of the Mood Elevator are made up of familiar feelings that people have told us are common for them.

My most common feeling is impatience. Can you relate to that? How does it show up for you? The traffic shouldn't be moving this slowly. The red light is lasting too long. The line I'm in is moving the slowest. The TV commercial is too long. We've talked long enough, let's just make the decision.

I've learned to recognize that impatient feeling. It is an uneasy feeling. I feel tense and far from relaxed. It is usually accompanied by irritation and bother. There is some intensity about it, and it can easily move into anger because I feel bottled up.

Worry has its own feeling too. It is usually not as intense as anger, but it can be even more unsettling. The easiest way for me to recognize worry is when I notice that the stories I am creating via my thoughts are going around and around – and my imaginary outcomes are becoming worse and worse.

Awareness or self-knowledge is the key to using your feelings as your guide. Understanding the Mood Elevator is useful. Carrying a reminder like a Mood Elevator pocket card (as I do) also helps create that awareness.

All mood states are accompanied by feelings. Which states are most common for you? Learning to read these signals early on is important, because the first step in managing mood states is to know when you are in one. Knowing where you are on the Mood Elevator is a prerequisite to utilizing many of the pointers in this book. You can learn to do that with awareness and practice.

■■■■■■■■■■■■■■■■

[which thoughts do you feed?]

"We become what we think about all day long."

– Ralph Waldo Emerson

Allow me to share a parable: One evening, an old Cherokee told his grandson about a conflict that goes on inside people. He said, "My son, the battle is between two wolves within us all. One is Evil. It is anger, envy, jealousy, sorrow, regret, worry, greed, arrogance, self-pity, guilt, resentment, inferiority, lies, false pride, superiority and ego. The other one is Good. It is joy, peace, love, hope, serenity, wisdom, humility, kindness, benevolence, empathy, generosity, truth, compassion and faith."

The grandson thought about this for a minute, and then asked his grandfather, "Which wolf wins?" The old Cherokee simply replied, "The one you feed."

We all have thoughts that take us to every level on the Mood Elevator, from top to bottom. We were given the gift of thought and the feelings that go along with it in order to experience life. The question is: Which kinds of thoughts do we feed and which dominate as a result? Sometimes we visit a mood level for just a moment which is natural and other times we camp out there for extended periods – something that's not helpful when it's a lower floor.

Worry can be a passing thought that comes and goes, or we can turn it into a full-length movie, like *Friday the 13th*, with all of the accompanying special effects.

When the new Senn Delaney consultant named Deborah mentioned in Chapter 2 learned she was going on a sales call with a CEO on short notice, she created a drama in her head in which she was fired, her son couldn't go to college and her family lost their house. She had low-level thinking and feelings in the days leading up to the CEO's visit. Despite her fears, it all went well and she even got some local consulting work out of it. Her worry served no purpose.

Worry is a great example of how we can feed our negative thoughts. Legitimate concerns can be useful in prompting us to be aware, take action or create a contingency plan. In contrast, they can also start us on a long and non-productive journey in our imagination.

Since our thinking creates our experience of life, we have the power to live in our own waking nightmares. Our thoughts are often like dominos: *Oh no! What about this? And then that might happen!* And so on.

I once had a worry habit that impacted my quality of life. I had mastered the art of embellishing my concerns, feeding my negative thoughts and projecting well beyond what was likely to happen. I found the key to changing was to catch my worry habit early on and learn to break the thought pattern before it got too far.

I began to notice when my worry was becoming a drama, when it was consuming too much of my thinking and when my spirits dropped for more than a brief time. Taking appropriate action when I could (or giving myself a gentle reminder, like "there you go again" or "don't go there") began to make a difference. Rather than feeding my worries, I learned to starve them.

When we get irritated, bothered or mad at someone, we can forgive quickly and let it go, or we can obsess about it and build a case in our head worthy of a prosecuting attorney presenting to the grand jury. The better we can understand that others are just doing what makes sense to them based on their thinking – flawed as it may be – the easier we can depersonalize the irritation and let it go.

Anger along with worry are the emotions we are most inclined to feed. When we are angry we also usually feel righteous. We feel we have been wronged. There is an injustice. It is not fair. Once we start the bonfire, we keep throwing wood (and sometimes even gasoline) on our thoughts to feed the flames.

While there may have been a wrong, anger rarely serves us; rather, it can consume us. The more we dwell on it the stronger the case we can build. We become blind to other possibilities or explanations. We don't hear well and often do and say things we later regret.

We need to starve – not feed – the flames of anger. The fuel is our escalating thoughts. The sooner we can break that spell we seem to be under when annoyed, the better off we (and those around us) will be. We all know from prior experience what works best for us to quiet our thinking: Walk away, take a break, engage in physical exercise, talk to a calm person you trust.

Feeling Depressed

Depression is a longer-term visit to lower quality thinking. It is an ongoing story we create through our thinking. In some people, it can be fueled by a chemical imbalance that can and often should be treated. For others, depression is simply a thought habit they get into often for understandable reasons. In the end it is our thinking and what we make of it that creates the persistent low mood.

I had one period in my life when I faced depression. It was almost 40 years ago after my first wife ended our marriage. She was my Sunday school sweetheart. We dated through college and then married. I thought our marriage would last forever.

When it didn't, I became dysfunctional for a time. The thinking I fueled was despair. Faith and hope got me to gradually shift my thinking. A wise friend I trusted sat me down and told me that while I couldn't see it now, I had a bright future. I was desirable and would love and be loved again. My sons loved me and I could create whatever relationship I wanted with them. That was in my hands.

I began to feed less despair into my projections of the future and have more thoughts of possibilities. I created a deep bond with my sons that still exists today. Rather than being the worst thing that happened in my life, my failed marriage turned out to be the best thing; it led to a richer, more fulfilling life. The shift from despair to hope happened via my thinking and my state of mind.

As you look at the bottom half of the Mood Elevator, which levels do you get caught up in projecting or embellishing?

- Are there specific things or people that irritate you?

- What brings out your impatience?

- What do you tend to dramatize?

- Do you have a worry habit?

- Are there people or things you are too judgmental about?

Like the wise Cherokee said, "the one you feed is the one that wins."

SOME LOWER STATES OF THE MOOD ELEVATOR

Impatient, Irritable

Bothered

Worried, Anxious

Defensive

Insecure, Not Good Enough

Jealous, Envious

Victimized, Blaming

Judgmental, Critical

Stressed, Burned-Out

Self-Righteous

Angry, Hostile

Sad, Lonely

Hopeless

Depressed

Now that you know what the lower states are, what are the clues you can look for to move yourself up the Mood Elevator? Use the concepts throughout this book to feed the thoughts and feelings you desire – and the others will diminish.

Chapter Seven

■■■■■■■■■■■■■■■■■

[the "stop" on the Mood Elevator]

With millions of real elevators in operation in buildings around the world, why is it that you never hear of one falling uncontrollably to the bottom? That only happens in horror movies (and in nightmares) because in addition to being safely built and inspected, all elevators have a mechanism – a "stop" in the form of a brake, or catch, that prevents them from falling even if a cable snaps. In a similar way, we can learn to activate a stop on our own Mood Elevator.

Where would you draw a line between the higher states and the lower states in the Mood Elevator?

THE MOOD ELEVATOR

grateful
wise, insightful
creative, innovative
hopeful, optimistic
patient, understanding
sense of humor
flexible, adaptive
curious, interested
impatient, frustrated
irritated, bothered
worried, anxious
defensive, insecure
judgmental, blaming
stressed, burned-out
depressed

Yes, the dividing line is "curious." And curiosity is the stop. It is handy because it is right in the middle – before we drop down into the lower mood states.

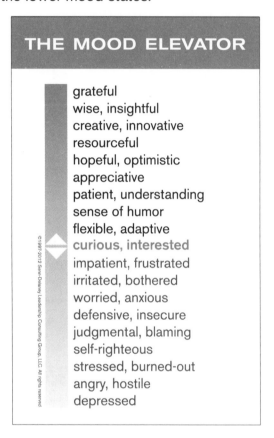

THE MOOD ELEVATOR

grateful
wise, insightful
creative, innovative
resourceful
hopeful, optimistic
appreciative
patient, understanding
sense of humor
flexible, adaptive
curious, interested
impatient, frustrated
irritated, bothered
worried, anxious
defensive, insecure
judgmental, blaming
self-righteous
stressed, burned-out
angry, hostile
depressed

Curiosity is an important level on the Mood Elevator because living life with more curiosity is a great way to avoid dropping to the lower floors. It is a useful and important "brake" in managing your moods. Here is how that works. When someone does something you don't understand or don't agree with, you can choose to be irritated, bothered, or judgmental. Or you can choose to be curious: *I wonder why they did that? I wonder why they see it that way?*

If someone says something you don't agree with, you can go

on the attack immediately by going to judgmental and defensive; or you can be curious. You can ask them to tell you more about why they see it that way and help you understand it from their point of view.

By being curious, you will get a different outcome – and a different feeling. No matter where you eventually end up in the conversation, you will always be further ahead if you begin with curious.

When life throws you a curve, you can go to angry or depressed mode or you can put your energy into what you can learn from the situation and what creative solutions might help get you out of it. This requires a curious mind.

To understand why curious is a "stop" on the Mood Elevator, take a quick look at the paragraph below. What thoughts immediately come to mind?

Those taht raed tihs hvae a sgtrane mnid. Olny 55 plepoe out of 100 can. I cdnuolt blveiee that I cluod aulaclty uesdnatnrd what I was rdanieg. The phaonmneal pweor of the hmuan mind. Aoccdrnig to rscheearch at Cmabrigde Uinervtisy, it dseno't mtaetr in what oerdr the ltteres in a word are, the olny iproamtnt tihng is that the frsit and last ltteer be in the rghit pclae. The rset can be a taotl mses and you can still raed it whotuit a pboerlm. This is bcuseae the huamn mnid deos not raed ervey lteter by istlef, but the wrod as a wlohe.

It is certainly an odd-looking paragraph. Did you try and read it? Were you one of about half of the population who can?

More importantly, where did your thinking go? Were you truly curious? Were you critical? Or did you ignore it because you didn't understand it? If you didn't read it, did you make it wrong?

If you made it wrong, you had lots of company. To some people, that paragraph just makes no sense. The spelling is awful and can be irritating to some. If that was you, you went to one of the most seductive and over-used lower levels of the Mood Elevator – judgment.

Now go back to that odd paragraph and try it again slowly. Read the last sentence first and it may start to make sense to you. If that doesn't work, take a look at it with the correct spelling below:

> Those that read this have a strange mind. Only 55 people out of 100 can. I could not believe I could actually understand what I was reading. The phenomenal power of the human mind. According to research at Cambridge University, it doesn't matter in what order the letters in a word are, the only important thing is that the first and last letter be in the right place. The rest can be a total mess and you can still read it without a problem. This is because the human mind does not read every letter, but the word as a whole.

This example is based on a scientific study to help understand how the mind works. How you viewed it does have implications. If you went to pure curiosity and exploration – congratulations! That might have shown up as a keen interest in trying to read it, or in wonderment about the fact that you could (or couldn't) read it. If you went too quickly to making it wrong, that might be a "judgment habit."

Here Comes the Judge

There are many reasons why people have a tendency to look at new and different things and go to judgment rather than curiosity. We get to be right because they are wrong. We are smart because we have the answer – and they don't. We want things to be correct according to our definition and interpretation of what is correct. When things don't fit, it is easier to make them wrong then to explore the unknown. If something doesn't fit our picture of how it should be, we invalidate it.

Our tendency to judge is why we get into heated discussions with people (including loved ones) about some of the most inconsequential things – things that really don't matter. It is why so many people see what is wrong with something, not what is right or what is different or what can be learned.

> "The highest form of intelligence is to observe without judgment."
>
> – Jiddu Krishnamurti

Too much judgment vs. curiosity and open-mindedness is the cause of many divorces and strained relationships. It is the reason most companies are not as agile or creative as they could be.

Even the most inventive people can fall prey to an "I'm smart and have the answer and you don't" mentality. When asked about the iPhone® while introducing Vista® in 2007, Microsoft CEO Steve Ballmer was completely dismissive in an interview with USA Today, saying, "There's no chance that the iPhone® is going to get any significant market share. No chance."

In the end, Vista was a flop, and Ballmer couldn't have been more wrong about the iPhone®. He couldn't accept the concept that people would work on screens without keypads. It didn't fit his picture. He would have been better off having a high level of curiosity about this new and different kind of phone, which went on to make billions of dollars for Apple.

You can choose to view life itself with curiosity. If something doesn't turn out the way you want it to, you can go to lots of lower floors on the Mood Elevator – or you can be curious. Ask yourself: How can I make lemonade out of lemons here? What can I learn from that? What's the best way to make the most of this? What is my role in all of it, and how might I need to grow or change?

I often tell people in our culture-shaping sessions that if they only have one "take away," let it be to live life in curiosity rather than judgment. If they do so they will have more satisfying relationships and a more successful and less stressful life.

So let go of any judgment habit you may have and let the curious floor on the Mood Elevator be a friend and a tool you use often.

"Look at everything as though you are seeing it for the first time, with eyes of a child, fresh with wonder."

– Joseph Cornell

[beware of unhealthy normal]

We do the best job of riding the Mood Elevator when we use our feelings as our guide. Unfortunately, there is a phenomenon that makes this more difficult to do. It is called "unhealthy normal." A metaphor to help understand unhealthy normal is the classic boiled frog syndrome story. As that story goes, if you put a frog in a pan of water and increase the heat very slowly, the frog gets used to every level; the frog won't notice the temperature changes – hence a boiled frog.

The frog is not "aware." It doesn't notice the water is getting dangerously hot. We can all be like the boiled frog when it comes to certain feelings. We become so accustomed to a lower-level feeling that we stop noticing it. We start out occasionally being bothered or irritated by people and events. We become more bothered by things and it becomes a habit we no longer even notice. That's "unhealthy normal." Our impatience escalates to irritation and then anger as our temperature goes up, and if we are not careful, constant impatience becomes our unhealthy normal. We are discerning or "realistic" and notice the negative side of things and then develop a habit or life outlook of being and feeling pessimistic.

At one point in my life excessive intensity was my unhealthy normal: I was overly concerned about getting everything done, doing it right, meeting my deadlines, not disappointing other people, being successful at everything that I did. I had become so accustomed to being wound up and intense that it became my norm. Only when I took a long-enough vacation, or really quieted my mind (like when I was in church), did I experience a more peaceful feeling – and I knew a different and calmer feeling state existed.

Unhealthy normal occurs when any lower-level mood state becomes so familiar that we don't notice it any more and it becomes our new norm. The problem is that if you don't notice it, you won't be prompted to do anything about it. Being judgmental or overly critical, living in a constant state of impatience, becoming easily irritated or bothered are all common levels of unhealthy normal. For some it can be insecurity with undue concern about how others feel about them. Others anger too easily. In each case the habit can become a way of life – and invisible.

It's like living right next to a busy highway for so long that you stop noticing the noise. That happened to me after Senn Delaney moved our headquarters into a new office building adjacent to the I-405 freeway near the Long Beach Airport (LGB) some years ago. The 405 is a busy, noisy freeway. When I first worked in the building, the constant sound of traffic bothered me. Today, when guests ask if I notice the noise, my response is, "What noise?"

Perhaps a better example is the California smog. Our oldest son, Kevin, is a famous kite boarder who is known as Top Hat;

he owns Hawaii Surf and Sail, a surf-oriented apparel store in Haleiwa on the legendary North Shore of Oahu. We love to visit Kevin and his wife whenever we can. With the constant trade winds, the sky on the North shore is a magnificent shade of blue. It is so clear, it is like watching High Definition TV with the bright pure white clouds floating in the deep blue sky. When we fly back into Los Angeles during daylight hours, I look down and say to myself, *Oh my gosh, I live in that smog?* The problem is that after I am back home for a week, I stop noticing the difference.

Unhealthy Normal and Relationships

When my wife's parents used to come visit us, she and I would notice how much they bickered. They would disagree about the most inconsequential things and constantly make each other wrong in little ways. We became aware of the subtle put downs or shots they took at one another. Obviously they were oblivious to it; it had become the invisible norm and they didn't notice it or see anything wrong with it.

Destructive, unhealthy normal mood states often arise in long-term relationships. Couples start to take each other for granted, stop communicating love and appreciation for each other and gradually, like the frog, start to lose touch with their feelings of love and affection.

The love that might have been blind to little faults at the start of a relationship turns into judgment about aspects of one another. Couples fail to see the innocence in each other's behaviors. They don't realize it is not about who is right or wrong, but about legitimate points of view based on a difference in personal filters and thinking.

In no area is the wise advice of "look to your feelings" more important than in close relationships. The feelings to watch for and cultivate are love, appreciation, forgiveness, non-judgment and compassion. When you keep these feelings alive, relationships flourish. The enemy of these feelings is when unhealthy normal becomes the norm in areas like judgment, fault-finding and the loss of feelings of warmth, love and acceptance.

George Pransky and his associates often work with couples to help them understand the three principles: mind, thought and consciousness. George tells the story of a couple that came for a four-day residential program because they felt that love was leaving their marriage. George helped them to see – not surprisingly – that their unhealthy normal was arguing, fighting and making each other wrong.

The couple left the retreat in a loving and hopeful state. But a week later, George got a panicked call from the husband, who said, "We've failed. We just had a fight and we are both so upset that we did." George replied, "Congratulations! You noticed this time, and you didn't like it. That's the best thing that could have happened." George went on to explain that when your undesirable behaviors and accompanying feelings become a loud bell that you then notice (and realize you are off base), things are most likely to get better.

What George was saying is that when your unhealthy normal is no longer invisible to you, you will start to change it. So long as you are unaware and unconscious about your unhealthy behavior, it will persist. That has been true for me. The excessive intensity I mentioned earlier is a good example. It was my unhealthy normal, and then it became a loud bell. When I started to notice it, I would take a deep breath and say to myself, *there you go again* or *be calm and be present.* Over time, my excessive intensity greatly diminished.

Unhealthy Normal in Organizations

Senn Delaney's work with corporate clients is to inspire, educate and partner with them to create healthy, high-performing organizational cultures. The first step in the work we do is to run what we call cultural diagnostics. We almost always discover unhealthy normal organizational habits in the process.

It takes an outsider to see these dysfunctions clearly because people who have been together awhile develop what could be called "familiarity blindness" or "cultural trances." It reminds me of the old adage, "We don't know who discovered water, but we know it wasn't the fish."

Familiarity blindness and cultural trances are organizational forms of unhealthy normal. Commonalities in habits can be found in any group; social scientist Kurt Lewin explained that this is because "the immediate social group is the largest determinant of behavior."

There are some definable and predictable unhealthy normal habits in organizations. Enron was an extreme and unfortunate example. Nowhere was a belief in self-interest more evident than at Enron. Before their collapse in 2001, Enron had been publicly recognized by McKinsey and Company and by business publications as an organization of the future that was bold, unconventional and – on paper, at least – highly profitable.

I met with executives at Enron years before their meltdown to explore ways that Senn Delaney could help them create an even more successful culture. Enron wanted more of what they had – extremely high expectations with an every-person-for-themselves, dog-eat-dog, results-at-any-cost mindset.

We didn't pursue the engagement because, as we told them, the survival-of-the-fittest, self-serving, non-collaborative, win-lose model they were creating was unsustainable.

It was an extreme case of the boiled frog as Enron pushed the limits of integrity and ethics to find "off-the-books" ways to keep the string of increasing quarterly earnings going. The few people within Enron who saw what was happening and tried to call it out became social outcasts as the unhealthy normal behavior became pervasive throughout the organization.

While Enron is an extreme example, lack of collaboration and decisions in self-interest vs. the greater good is perhaps the most common dysfunctional organizational habit. Senn Delaney saw that early on in our work to help transform the culture of the regional Bell phone companies after divestiture.

Bell Atlantic was our first Telco (i.e., telephone) client. They were made up of state phone companies on the Atlantic seaboard. Their CEO, Ray Smith, knew he needed to quickly convert a monopolistic, state-centric company into a collaborative global competitor.

Senn Delaney knew we had a challenge during our needs assessment when Bell Atlantic employees told us that it was common for one state phone company division to celebrate if another state phone company lost a rate case with the regulators because it made them look better by comparison. Since rates that the regulators granted have a big impact on profits, the loss by, say, Pennsylvania would make New Jersey look better in the internal comparisons. This happened even though everyone knew they were the same company with just one stock price.

Another unconscious organizational habit is "the blame game" or "it wasn't my fault or my job." The negative impact of this unconscious habit struck me early on in developing Senn Delaney's culture-shaping model. Our retail-consulting group was doing some projects for the JL Hudson department stores in Detroit. One engagement was to improve performance in their Warren Distribution Center, where goods were received from vendors, checked, marked, sorted and then sent off to the stores.

Hudson's was a part of the Dayton Hudson Corporation with Target and others, and their distribution center was by far the worst in the group. We couldn't find anything wrong with the plant layout, equipment, systems or processes. What we *did* find in our interviews was an almost terminal case of lack of accountability. Everyone said there was a problem – but then pointed to someone else as the cause of it. The markers blamed the checkers, the checkers blamed the buyers and the buyers blamed the vendors.

Blaming and excuses were so prevalent and so ingrained that no one could see the real problem. It was just unhealthy normal. In a leadership session with the distribution team we surfaced their "victim" habit and replaced it with a mindset of accountability. That led to the Warren Distribution Center becoming the best performer in the Dayton Hudson group.

The blame game can become a habit for individuals, whole organizations, families and couples. If life partners engage in blame, it can be very destructive.

We are taught from childhood through sports and in games that for me to win, you have to lose. That thinking shows up in organizations but also in families and with couples, where it takes the form of the need for one partner to be right while making the other wrong. When that becomes an unconscious habit, relationships suffer and marriages can end.

Who is right and who was supposed to do what is the center of many fights with most couples. The fact is, there are always two sides to every story and some degree of joint accountability. Unless someone is willing to say, "Yes I did it" or "I am wrong" or at least, "We both had a role in this," the relationship gets damaged.

In all of these examples you can use your feelings as your guide – so long as those feelings haven't become unhealthy normal. Learn to recognize your unhealthy feelings. You'll know you are off base if you feel righteous, judgmental, angry, irritated or bothered. Make these feelings like a loud bell – and when you hear that bell ring, you'll know that your thinking is unreliable and must proceed with caution.

How do you make your feelings a loud bell? Start by seeing if you can identify any unhealthy normal tendencies you might have from this list:

Unhealthy Normal Habit Candidates

Impatience

Pessimism

Irritation or Bother

Anger

Anxious

Worry

Excessive Intensity

Judgment

Insecure

Unworthy

Needy

Need to be right

Argumentative

Self-Righteous

Disconnected

Blaming or Excuses (it's not my fault)

Difficulty in admitting mistakes or saying I was wrong

We also develop unhealthy patterns of thought that can impact our moods. The work of Amy Farabaugh, PhD, an Assistant Professor of Psychiatry at Harvard Medical School, established a link between thought habits and physical and mental health. Farabaugh suggests we learn to recognize and challenge our unhealthy patterns of thought. Her research shows this will reduce our risk of physical and mental health problems, and increase our life span.

The chart below explains thought patterns originally published in *Mind, Mood & Memory* by Massachusetts General Hospital (July 2011).

PATTERNS OF THOUGHT

Selective thinking: focusing on negative details of situations and ignoring positive aspects

All-or-nothing thinking: situations are seen in stark absolutes – success or failure, black or white, good or bad, perfect or disastrous

Personalizing situations: unnecessarily assuming that events involve you, or taking responsibility for things over which you have little or no control

Overgeneralizing: drawing conclusions on the basis of a single incident, or without sufficient evidence, instead of seeing the big picture

Catastrophizing: magnifying the negative aspects of a situation or expecting the worst possible outcome

---

Mind, Mood & Memory by Massachusetts General Hospital (July 2011)

Each of these patterns comes with a set of feelings. What lower mood states and which unhealthy normal thought patterns have you developed? If you recognize any unhealthy patterns in your life, learning to catch the feeling early can be useful. We'll explore ways to do that in later chapters.

Chapter Nine

[doing "down" well]

ave you ever had a down day, low feelings or moments when life didn't look so good? Of course you have. Having low moods is a very natural and normal part of life. The pointers and tips in the book are designed to help minimize the duration and frequency of your time in the lower states. But we all will spend time there. That's why a second goal of this book is to help you do less damage to yourself and others when you are feeling down.

Human beings are unique in the animal kingdom because we have the power of thought. This allows us to imagine the future, plan for things that have yet to come, imagine possibilities and analyze and interpret everything that is going on within and around us. Thought has allowed us to put a man on the moon, conquer polio, write ageless classical music and simply plan and envision our next vacation.

That same power to imagine through thought can also cause us to worry excessively and unnecessarily, experience periods of depression about real or imagined conditions in life, have moments of paranoia in assuming the motives of others, be self-righteous and judgmental and even have fits of anger and rage.

I know from personal experience that the concepts in this book, when applied, can allow you to spend more of your time in the higher mood states, reaping the benefits of that higher quality thinking. I also know that no matter how well you understand these principles, your thinking will at times take you to the lower levels of the Mood Elevator. That's why learning to "do down well" is such a necessary skill.

Given that, how does one "do down well?"

Have you ever said something to a friend or loved one in the heat of the moment and later wished you could have taken it back? While there may have been a grain of truth in what you said, chances are you over-reacted, over-stated it, misinterpreted it, or were totally off the mark. If so, where were you on the Mood Elevator? Most likely you were somewhere in the lower half.

When working with business groups on the Mood Elevator, we ask, "Have you ever sent an email, perhaps in response to one you received, that you wished you could have taken back?" Most everyone agrees that they have, and were down the Mood Elevator when they did so.

When I get an email that "pushes my button," I may type a response – but then I will hit "save to draft." When I read my reply again (usually hours later or the next day), I sometimes just delete it and start over. More often than not, I'll add things like "Thanks for pointing that out" and edit the message to take the irritation and judgment out of it before finally hitting "send."

Thinking is Unreliable in Low Mood States

Saying things to a loved one you don't really mean and sending an over-reactive email both illustrate the most important principle to doing down well: *Know that your thinking is unreliable in the lower mood states.* Don't trust it; try not to act on it right away.

When we are excessively worried, angry, self-righteous or depressed, our thinking is almost always faulty. Since faulty thinking leads to inappropriate words and deeds, it follows that we should be very cautious in our actions and words when we are in the lower mood states.

We often ask groups we work with if anyone has ever had a useful, fruitful dialogue with a loved one when both parties were in the basement of the Mood Elevator. The universal answer is "No." While people might eventually sort through it, no one (to date) has ever said they have had a constructive and useful conversation when both parties were in a lower state of mind.

Relationships can be torn apart by things people do and say when they are in lower mood states such as anger, self-righteousness or judgment. My wife, Bernadette, and I have been together more than 30 years – and we had some unproductive arguments while in lower mood states before we gained this understanding. We first got together in the 1970s – the era of the human potential movement. Conventional wisdom at the time was "Tell it like it is" and "Don't go to bed at night with anything left unsaid." There were a few times we struggled unproductively until all hours.

As we both began to better understand how the Mood Elevator works, Bernadette suggested a new ground rule: Let's not take on any issues if either of us is in the lower states of the Mood Elevator. The results of that new ground rule on our relationship have been quite remarkable. It is one reason we have a much more loving, respectful relationship today. We take on issues and stay free of hidden agendas – but we do so when we are both in the higher mood states.

It often goes like this. I may say to her, "It looks like you are bothered; is it something you want to talk about?" Her reply often is, "No, not now. My thinking is not clear. If I need to talk about it, I'll let you know later." Bernadette knows her momentary thinking may be unreliable because of how she is feeling, and she understands that if the concern doesn't look different when she is back "up," we can discuss it better when we are both in a healthy place. When we do find a good time to talk about it, the issue is usually dealt with very easily and in an almost "by the way" manner. I believe that is one of our keys to a loving relationship without the all-too-common arguing and bickering many couples have.

Remarkably, our 12-year-old son, Logan, somehow understands it best. He does have his occasional meltdown when he is overwhelmed with homework or having a bad day. When he does, he tells us, "Don't try to talk to me now. Just leave me alone because I won't hear you anyway. I don't want to talk to you now because if I do, I'll say something I really don't mean. Just let me go to my room, leave me alone until I'm back to the real me and then I'll come out again." He goes to his room, immerses himself in games that calm his thinking and waits until the mood passes. Many adults could benefit from a similar approach to their moods.

One of our consultants at Senn Delaney came up with a great analogy for doing down well. He said that if you *had* to go out on a very icy and snowy night, you would do so – but with great caution. You would drive more slowly, take turns more gently and slow down before getting close to any obstacles.

That's a useful analogy to remember when you're having a bad day or when you get caught in a low mood. Just know that your instincts are not right. It is not a time to tell a loved one, friend, employee or colleague what you think of them – no matter how much you want to do so. It is *not* a time to make any important life decisions. It is *not* a time to deal with any issues you have with others. Instead, like my son Logan, just wait until your natural health re-emerges on the upper floor of the Mood Elevator, and then deal with the situation. You will find that you can deal with issues much more easily, quickly and painlessly.

In fact, when you feel the most passionate and intense about telling someone what you think of him or her, or discussing something they did that you didn't like – *don't!* When you feel compelled to take someone including a loved one on – *don't!* Wait until you calm down. Chances are good that you will say it differently, and they will hear it better.

To be human means there are times for joy and times for sorrow; times to laugh and times to cry; times to be confident and times to be insecure; times to be loving and times to be angry. That is why the promise of this book is not to help you to always be "up," but to assist you in living more of your life in the upper states of the Mood Elevator while doing less damage to yourself and others when down.

Using the Mood Elevator as your guide and not acting on low-level thoughts and impulses when you are feeling down is one of the key principles to doing less damage to yourself – and to others.

[SHIFTING YOUR SET POINT ON THE MOOD ELEVATOR]

part two

Chapter Ten

■■■■■■■■■■■■■■■■

[taking care of yourself, part 1: resting the body, quieting the mind]

The benefits of living life up the Mood Elevator are obvious. But, how can we do it with greater grace and ease? What else can we do to impact our moods in addition to understanding the role of thought?

I have found that there are two practices that can move your "set point" up the Mood Elevator. All people have a "set point" when it comes to body temperature. Most people have a set point for their weight as well (It's the number you fluctuate around and keep coming back to.) We also tend to have a set point on the Mood Elevator.

People who adopt these practices and shift their set point are more resilient; spending more time higher up the Mood Elevator. They don't slide down the elevator as easily and when they do the duration is often not as long.

The first practice is the easiest to understand and perhaps the best documented. Given our busy lives we just don't do it. It is simply taking better care of ourselves physically.

Take Better Care of Yourself

Learning to take better care of yourself will shift your set point on the Mood Elevator and improve the way you ride it. We all know we do better when we are fit and rested but few are as intentional about maintaining that fitness as they could be. It is as simple as this; when you are rested and more relaxed you are more resilient. It's harder for other people to push your buttons and you are not as easily irritated or bothered. That's because there is a connection between our physical state and our mental resilience. For most people, life looks better after a good night's sleep, a weekend off work, or a more restful vacation.

Studies have shown that we catch colds more easily when we are run down. Our physical immune system is weakened. A parallel phenomenon exists with moods. When we get run down and tired, it is easier for our thinking to go south. We are more sensitive to what other people say and take things more personally. We are less patient and understanding and often feel overwhelmed.

Since the quality of our thinking is lower when we are tired, we are not as wise and resourceful. Our effectiveness is hampered and that compounds the perceived stress and pressure we feel.

In contrast, when we are more rested, our thinking tends to be more reliable and less susceptible to creating those bad movies in our head and the stress that goes with it. That stress is a result of our thinking and our thinking is impacted by our physical state. Fortunately, there are specific ways to "take better care of yourself" so you will be more resilient and less apt to slide down the Mood Elevator.

The Importance of Stretch and Recover Cycles

The foundation of best practices that help you take better care of yourself is an understanding of the body and mind's need to both stretch and recover or renew. The human body was designed to stretch and recover but we often forget the recover part. Weight lifters understand recovery: they work one part of the body very hard to break down their muscles and then they let that body part rest the next day so it grows and becomes stronger.

Tennis players also have recovery rituals such as playing with their ratchet strings and bouncing the ball between vigorous sets and serves. They play the game with great bursts of energy and brief recover times.

After being a jogger for decades I decided to take up triathlons several years ago so I could cross train. By running one day and biking or swimming the next I use different muscles while other muscle groups rest and recover.

Jim Loehr and Tony Schwartz wrote a best-selling book a few years back entitled *The Power of Full Engagement: Managing Energy, Not Time, is the Key to High Performance and Personal Renewal*. They make the case that great performances from top athletes and peak-performing individuals require that they stretch and recover. Stretching means going beyond our comfort zone to expand us mentally, emotionally and physically. Levels on the Mood Elevator like curious, inspired, optimistic, innovative, resourceful and determined all help us stretch.

Man was meant to live life in cycles. To live life at the fullest and at our best, we need to create our own "cycles" of stretch and recover in many aspects of our lives. Physical fitness is one of those areas; it greatly impacts our energy levels. We can use aerobic exercise, stretching, yoga and resistance training to build our stamina and energy levels.

Stretch and recover is relevant in mental fitness as well. More and more research shows that stretching our minds adds brain cells and wards off mental decline in later years. Rest through meditation also impacts how our brain functions.

Having a growth mindset helps promote the "stretch" part of stretch and recover. That involves learning new things, taking on challenging assignments and calculated risks – both professionally and interpersonally.

But we can only stretch for so long before burning out. So we also need ways to recover. Recovery includes sleep, rest and time spent in some renewing, higher-mood states such as grateful, loving, peaceful and humorous.

Sleep

"The best bridge between despair and hope is a good night's sleep."

– E. Joseph Cossman

The most important recovery mechanism people have is to simply get enough sleep. That's why there is night and day and the circadian cycles. And yet in our nonstop 24/7 internet-driven world the majority of us are sleep deprived.

Sleep deprivation makes us vulnerable to sliding down the Mood Elevator. It also has been associated with numerous medical problems including obesity, diabetes, high blood pressure, stroke, cardiovascular disease and depression.

When we have a lack of sleep we can't complete puzzles, take tests or solve problems as well. Research has shown we lose points of IQ and are not as smart. We also lose points of EQ, have less access to creative original thought and our ability to handle stressful situations and deal with people suffers.

Researchers at the University of Warwick in Coventry and University College London found that lack of sleep can more than double the risk of death from cardiovascular disease. According to Professor Francesco Cappuccio, MD *"Short sleep has been shown to be a **risk factor** for weight gain, hypertension and Type 2 diabetes, sometimes leading to mortality."*

Sleep difficulties are closely associated with psychiatric disorders such as depression, alcoholism and bipolar disorder. Up to 90% of adults with depression are found to have sleep difficulties.

Sleep provides time for our body and mind to recover. The mind slows, especially during deep non-rapid eye movement (NREM) sleep. It shifts from alpha to delta waves, which are therapeutic and restful. The importance of NREM sleep can be seen in studies where people were denied deep sleep. If denied sleep for too long, subjects became psychotic and experienced hallucinations and paranoid schizophrenic thoughts.

The right kind of sleep is also important to learning, gaining insights and in decision making. All of the conscious and unconscious events and images we have taken in during the day are stored in the brain. During sleep the brain processes all that and puts it together.

Rebecca Spencer PhD, professor of psychology at the University of Massachusetts, says, *"REM sleep is good for problem solving and decision making because your brain is putting pieces together and trying new alternatives. You gain insights that wouldn't occur to you when you were awake".*

She also says REM activates the emotional area of the brain so "that the things that are most important to you on a gut level are prioritized." In a research test, groups took part in an experiential exercise or game that had a hidden underlying rule.

One group had a chance to sleep on it before debriefing the game the next morning. The other group played the game in the morning and debriefed it later that day. Twice as many people who slept on it figured out the rule. They got deeper insights and were more perceptive about it.

Senn Delaney has found something similar in our culture-shaping sessions for teams of executives. While a one-day session can provide value, a two-day session with evening reflection and sharing the second morning is much more transformational.

> "It is a common experience that a problem difficult at night is resolved in the morning after the committee of sleep has worked on it."
>
> – John Steinbeck

Sleep in and of itself can provide a mood lift. We've all had the experience of feeling low or depressed or overwhelmed with the challenges of the day. A good restful night's sleep can make the whole world look better. When rested we feel stronger and more capable. We also have more complete access to our wisest self.

Recovery is About Finding That Quieter Mind

In addition to sleep, "recovery" also means some restful time away from whatever your role or task is in life — be it a career or as a homemaker. We need to find other ways in the course of our daily life to quiet our mind.

That has become increasingly difficult in this iPhone®, iPad®, smart phone everywhere broadband world. Information comes at us constantly. I met a CEO recently who said he expected to get a response back within 30 minutes from anyone on his senior team 24 hours a day, 7 days a week. While this is extreme, more and more people do respond to text messages and emails as they arrive whenever that is.

Vacation is not relaxing time off if we are constantly on the alert for incoming information. The same can be said for weekends and holidays.

Finding Time to Just Be

Higher quality thinking has a different feel than lower quality thinking. In the higher mood states our thoughts are more flowing, clearer and not frenzied. Feelings like gratitude, love, peace and calm come with almost no effort in thinking. They are what could be called being states. Spending time there provides recovery time.

We know we are truly in the moment "being here now" when we are overwhelmed by a beautiful scene in nature or by the pure love of a child. During those times our mind is quiet and our thoughts are still.

It is much like an undisturbed flowing river: the river of life. When we are at our best, the surface is calm even though lots of water is running underneath.

In contrast, when we are down the Mood Elevator our thinking is cloudy and less clear. We can get caught up in thoughts of worry, anger, insecurity and judgment; thinking that tends to go around and around and spiral downward. It is as if a tree was felled at the bank of our river of life and the current is now swirling around and around, disturbing the calm surface with what I call "mental eddies." Learning to recognize and calm those mental eddies helps de-stress our lives.

Two techniques help me find those quieter moments. One is to compartmentalize my work time and my off time. And, yes, I do often take some work home at night, on weekends and on vacation. The trick is to not be *mentally* at work all the time.

I turn my smart phone off during my son's volleyball games, most evenings and during large blocks of my weekend and vacation off time. I allocate brief blocks of time to catch up on emails but then turn off my smart phone and hopefully also turn off much of my thinking about work. It helps to not constantly check my email or my smart phone. This provides not only recovery time for me but also more quality time with my loved ones.

"Be Here Now" Time

The answer to that quality time is something we teach in our sessions called *Be Here Now*. It is the ability to be fully present in the moment with a quieter mind. We are usually so caught up in our thinking that special moments in life pass us by.

Have you ever been with a person but you were not there? Conversely, have you ever been with a person and you knew they were not there? Have you ever had a day off but your working mind never shut down? Have you gone on a vacation but only your body made it there? Have you ever had what could have been quiet time but instead your mind kept racing and you never fully relaxed? All of these are examples of not being here now in the present moment. They are also lost opportunities to refresh, renew and recover.

Human beings spend a substantial amount of time thinking about things other than what they are doing at the moment. Although "mind wandering" has been credited as having a role in learning, reasoning and planning, many philosophical and religious traditions teach that happiness is to be found by living in the present moment.

In an article in *Harvard Science* magazine entitled "A Wandering Mind is not a Happy Mind", Harvard psychologists Matthew Killingsworth and Daniel Gilbert investigated the relationship between a wandering mind and happiness in the real world. They developed a Web application for the iPhone® that allowed them to randomly sample the emotional status, activities and mind state of about 5000 people from 83 different countries. They found we spend at least half of our time thinking about something other than our immediate surroundings – and most of this thinking does not make us happy.

The results showed that:

1. People are less happy when their minds are wandering than when they are not, regardless of their current activity; and

2. What people are thinking is a better predictor of their happiness than what they are doing.

The Role of Breathing in a Quieter Mind

The second technique I employ to find those peaceful, centering moments is a simple and quick way to quiet my mind and be more present when I'm on the go and in the midst of a hectic day. It turns out that the key is in our breathing. Research has found that slow deep breathing somehow triggers the parasympathetic nervous system which induces calm.

Simple as it sounds, the technique is merely to stop, take a deep breath or two and say to myself as I let the air out "Be Here Now." That somehow has a centering effect and clears my thoughts – at least for the moment. It works great when I'm going from one meeting to another or before walking in the door when I get home at night.

I was first introduced to the power of breathing when I read a book by Dr. Herbert Benson, MD, of the Harvard Medical School called *The Relaxation Response*. Benson studied eastern techniques of meditation including use of mantras, and found merely repeating a neutral word like **one** each time you exhaled for several minutes while in a relaxed position quieted the mind. He was able to document through research that it also reduced pulse rate and blood pressure. I've proven this myself by being able to drop my resting pulse rate to as low as 53 when it is normally around 60 and my blood pressure to 90 over 50 (when it is usually 20 to 30 points higher.)

I have used the relaxation response and variants of that technique for years to start my day or to quiet my mind before going to sleep. More recently I was introduced to author and psychologist John Selby who has spent much of his life developing ways to help people de-stress and perform at their best by accessing the genius within via a quieter mind. Selby also points to the power of breathing but with a twist.

His theory is that if you give the mind two or more tasks to perform it can't wander – hence a quieter mind. In practice he recommends breathing through the nose while noticing the air as it moves in and out. If that is not enough to quiet your mind the second simultaneous task is to notice the rise and fall of your chest or stomach. The concentration required to do both of these things at once makes other more complex thinking more difficult resulting in a quieter mind.

Studies have shown that meditation increases the thickness of regions of the brain that control attention and process sensory signals from the outside world. Amishi P. Jha, PhD, at the University of Miami, runs a program called "Mindfulness based mind-fitness training." Like Selby's and Benson's process, Jha relies on quieting the mind through focus. Jha explains that mindfulness training has demonstrated it can enhance mental agility and attention "by changing brain structure and function so the brain processes are more efficient" – the quality associated with higher intelligence.

In the midst of a busy day, a practical short cut to a quieter mind for me is to take a few deep breaths through my nose whenever I feel I am ramping up, becoming too intense or need to really be here now for a person or a meeting. We have all experienced this on occasion. We are rushed and stressed and we almost involuntarily let out a big sigh. That is our body's way of relaxing.

The payoff in all this is less stress, a clearer more creative mind and a shift in your set point on the Mood Elevator. When we are rested and more relaxed we are more resilient and it's harder for other people to push our buttons. We are not as easily irritated when we have a quieter mind. Try these techniques and see if they make a difference for you. It works even better when you add the pointers in the next chapter of taking care of yourself.

Chapter Eleven

■■■■■■■■■■■■■■■■

[taking care of yourself, part 2: exercise and diet]

"use it or lose it"

Exercise plays a major role in mental fitness and in our set point on the Mood Elevator. There are some physiological reasons for this: Exercise increases our blood flow and builds our stamina so we don't tire as easily. Vigorous exercise tends to clear our head; that is, it rids us of that circular thinking. It also produces endorphins, which are like a safe, legal narcotic that gives us a positive feeling.

Exercise can provide benefits in three aspects of your life: the physical, the mental and the emotional. A meta-analysis of over 100 studies on the impact of exercise was published in the *American Journal of Psychiatric Health*. The researchers concluded that "Exercise improves mental heath and well-being, reduces stress and anxiety and enhances cognitive functioning."

In their book, *Well Being: The Five Essential Elements*, Tom Rath and Jim Harter from Gallup say that even 20 minutes of exercise a day gives people a more positive outlook on life. I also have found this to be true. If I can get in even a brief run early in the morning before work, it raises my spirits and starts my day with a clearer mind and fresher point of view.

In my case, exercise also does something else. Many of the ideas for *Up the Mood Elevator* came to me while I was out jogging. When I start my run, the first thing that happens is that my head begins to clear and my busy mind starts to slow down. Once that happens, fresh thoughts begin to occur to me. I'm not sure where they come from, but they are almost always more inspiring and interesting thoughts than the ones I have while sitting at my computer typing out text.

Exercise is a vital component of any plan to live a healthier and longer life. My interest in running developed decades ago when I read Ken Cooper MD's original book, *Aerobics*. Cooper was the first person to popularize the notion that there was a connection between aerobic exercise and cardiovascular health. Prior to that, bed rest and a sedentary life was the prescription for those with heart problems.

Cooper's theory was "use it or lose it," and hundreds of studies have documented the validity of that premise. His Cooper Clinic in Dallas continues to do great research on the connection between exercise and heart disease. They have proven that even those who exercise moderately have measurably less chance of heart problems than sedentary people.

I had been in pretty good shape as a basketball player in high school, a gymnast in college and recreational league basketball player into my late 20s. Then I got busy starting a consulting business and raising three kids – and I stopped exercising much. As a result, I packed on 35 pounds.

I got my wake-up call after reading Cooper's book *Aerobics*. It contained a self-administered fitness test in the back, and had been designed by Cooper for use with the military. The test was a simple one: Run as far as you can in 12 minutes. The test is meant to measure the condition of the person taking it. The outcome is based on the distance the test person ran, their age and gender. (The results can be correlated with VO_2 Max.) I made it a couple of blocks before I was gasping for air with an ache in my side. I knew I was out of shape and in trouble. I failed the test miserably.

Cooper's book had a table of equivalents – how much walking vs. running vs. tennis or racquetball it took to get and stay aerobically fit. My family and I got a membership to a racquetball club, but I found with my frequent travel, running was a more practical and efficient exercise for me.

That was almost 40 years ago and, like Forrest Gump, I haven't stopped running since. To save my knees, I began cross-training with road biking and swimming several years ago. That led to my current passion for sprint triathlons. The weight came off and stayed off as I continued to do my regular exercise and slowly changed to a healthier diet.

Aerobics, along with the research I have seen over the years since, made me a firm believer that the body doesn't wear out; it rusts out from lack of use. Recent studies by Art Kramer, PhD, of the University of Illinois at Urbana-Champaign, found that simple aerobic exercise (such as vigorous walking 45 minutes, three days a week) improved memory by 20 percent. A more dramatic finding was that a year of intense exercise can give a 70-year-old the mental functioning of a 30-year-old – with improved memory, planning skills, the ability to deal with ambiguity and handle simultaneous tasks.

As Kramer says, "You can think of fitness training as changing the molecular and cellular building blocks that underlie many cognitive skills."

One of the biggest payoffs of regular aerobic exercise is increased energy and stamina. This directly contributes to staying up the Mood Elevator.

Exercise Beyond Aerobics

There are three forms of exercise that make sense to me. Of these, the first and most important is aerobic exercise – which gets the heart rate up and provides all the benefits described above. The second is anaerobic exercise – which is simply resistance or strength training. It, too, contributes to vitality and stamina.

Strengthening the muscles, especially our core, contributes to a more satisfying life. When we work our core muscles, we also exercise our abdominals. Strengthening our abs not only keeps our stomachs from growing with age, but also protects our backs. And that reduces the aches and pains that can take us down the Mood Elevator.

Resistance training also increases our metabolism and contributes to weight loss or weight maintenance as we age. It also builds bone density. It enables us to engage in more vigorous activities without having physical limitations. This contributes to a better quality of life and the quality of our thinking. It also helps give us the energy to face life's challenges with more confidence.

A 2010 study published in the *Archives of Internal Medicine* found that as little as one or two resistance sessions a week for a period of a year improved mental acuity and cognitive performance.

The third and perhaps most neglected exercise is stretching. In Chapter 11, we talked about the idea of "stretch and recover" as it applies to life. Stretching out of our comfort zone in new directions expands us mentally and emotionally, and recovery time centers us and helps keep us at our best.

But the body also needs to stretch and recover. Running, walking and other aerobic exercise keeps your cardiovascular system more open and flexible. Strength training breaks down your muscles, and recovery time repairs in a stronger state.

As we age, our joints and tendons contract and we become less flexible. We need to apply the same "stretch and recover" model to joints and tendons too. Yoga is a great way to stretch as well as quiet the mind. (I'm not into it, but I should be.) I do, however, stretch regularly, and am driven by an image in my head of what happens when I don't. I live a few miles from a retirement community in Seal Beach, California called Leisure World; sometimes I go to the shopping center nearby. I have seen some of the elderly people trying to back their cars out of parking places. Their biggest challenge? They can't turn their necks far enough to see what's behind them. That picture – plus images of people I have known with back problems – provides incentive to me to stretch my neck, back and hamstrings regularly.

Many people report that they are mentally more creative and stable when they exercise regularly and take care of themselves. That's why regular exercise is one of the long-term answers to raising your set point on the Mood Elevator.

In the short term, try getting a good night's sleep, taking a 10-minute walk during a break at work, or calling for a stretch break in a meeting. All of these things tend to elevate the spirit.

If you want to have more success with less stress, to live life more in the higher states of the Mood Elevator and be less reactive when you are down, make a plan for how you are going to take better care of yourself through exercise.

The Food We Eat

Hundreds of books have been written on diet and nutrition. I don't plan to compete with that in a book about the Mood Elevator. But make no mistake – there is a direct link between what you eat, how physically fit you are and how well you do on the Mood Elevator. It's all a part of taking care of *you*.

The biggest issue with the typical American diet is that it puts on weight and damages the cardiovascular system, leading to heart disease, stroke, erectile dysfunction and other ailments that slow us down and reduce our quality of life.

Several popular reality shows, including *The Biggest Loser*, have been watched by millions of people. And still, we have an obesity epidemic in America. Nearly one-third of the population fall into the obese category and nearly 60 percent of people are overweight.

While diets work for a few, most don't work for the majority of people in the long term. The best chance of eating right for health and weight is to find healthful foods you can eat as a permanent lifestyle – not as a short-term diet. The key is to learn what foods you should and shouldn't eat, and then within the healthy ones find what you can stick with indefinitely. Without this knowledge people with weight issues face a lifetime of yo-yo dieting with one meal plan or fad after another. Each may make a difference short term but without knowledge and a lifestyle change, the weight comes back.

I am not a medical doctor nor am I a trained dietician, but I have read dozens of studies on health and nutrition, and tried many of the recommendations while tracking my results with blood panels and subjective measures of weight gain, energy and stamina.

My journey toward healthy eating habits started around the time I failed my Cooper aerobics test. I had a regular check up with my family doctor, which included a simple blood test. My physician casually mentioned that my cholesterol was a little high and that "you might switch from whole milk to low fat." This was the 70s, and very little had been written to date about cholesterol and heart disease. I looked up all the references I could find, and a pattern began to emerge.

It seems that saturated fats in particular contribute to blocked arteries. The case was best stated first by Nathan Pritikin. His 1975 book, *Live Longer Now: The First One Hundred Years of Your Life*, started me on my dietary journey. Nathan Pritikin was not a medical doctor nor nutritionist either; he was an engineer who owned several companies in fields such as electronics and photography. He held numerous patents in these fields. His interest in health matters began in earnest when he found out that he suffered from heart disease, and he used his investigative ability to solve that problem, just as he had solved many others.

In 1957, when he was 40 years old, Pritikin was diagnosed as having serious heart disease. Based on what the doctors told him at the time, he was faced with a lifetime of drugs and ever-increasing restrictions on his physical movements. He couldn't accept that passive prescription, so he exhausted the scientific literature and created a diet and exercise program to treat his disease. After nine years of trial and error, he cured himself.

Pritikin's research made him aware of the link between fat consumption and atherosclerosis, or hardening of the arteries. He learned that countries where people consume the most fat had the most arterial disease. He found other interesting clues: During World War II, arterial disease diminished drastically all across Europe because fatty foods were in short supply. Pritikin became convinced that somewhere there was an answer to this puzzle – and he set out to find it.

Long before most doctors and scientists were willing to acknowledge that something as simple as diet might be causing serious illnesses, Pritikin had, on his own accord, created a program to treat people, using food and exercise as medicine. It was a revolutionary departure from the current medical thinking of the time.

For 10 years, he tested his program on relatives, friends, and friends of friends and in 1976 he opened the *Pritikin Longevity Center* in Santa Barbara, California. Its successes against illnesses such as heart disease, diabetes, arthritis and gout (as well as many others) proved to be greater than even Pritikin had dreamed. Eighty-five percent of those who came to the Center on medication for high blood pressure left with normal blood pressure and no medication; half of adult-onset diabetics left insulin-free; more than half of those who came to the center already scheduled for heart bypass surgery left never needing the operation. Thousands upon thousands of people who arrived at the center unable to walk even a block without pain, left able to walk – even run – for miles at a stretch.

The diet plan Pritikin created was high in whole grains, vegetables and dietary fiber and very low in fats. Fewer than 10 percent of total calories came from fats.

At the time he developed his diet, Pritikin's concepts seemed quite radical. In fact, Pritikin was ahead of his time, and today – despite a few controversies along the way – most of his principles have been incorporated into advice given on how to reduce the risk of developing cardiovascular disease by such mainstream organizations as the American Heart Association.

Pritikin died in 1985 of causes unrelated to his cardiovascular system, and upon autopsy doctors discovered no signs of heart disease – a fact they attributed to his rigorous, life-long adherence to his diet.

That information, along with other studies, prompted me to begin to reduce the saturated fat in my diet and increase the vegetables, fruits and high-fiber whole grains. I later learned that saturated fats (like those found in animal products) are bad for you, and unsaturated fats (like the Omega 3 oils found in olive oil and fatty fish like salmon) are good for you. I also learned about the power of antioxidants found in certain berries.

Studies continue to be published linking diet to disease. The strongest link, I think, is to animal products – red meat in particular. In a 2011 report by researchers at the Harvard School of Public Health, decade-long data from over 400,000 people showed that just a small 2-ounce serving a day of processed meat (like hot dogs, bacon or lunch meat) increased the risk of diabetes by 50 percent, while just 4 ounces of any red meat (such as hamburger or steak) increased diabetes by 20 percent. Substituting nuts and whole grains lowered the risk of Type 2 diabetes by up to 35 percent.

A Canadian study helped validate the impact of cholesterol-busting foods. Just a handful of almonds or walnuts each day, along with the substitution of soy products for milk products, reduced LDL ("bad") cholesterol significantly.

A National Institutes of Health and AARP study found that men who ate the most red meat had a 31 percent higher overall death rate that those who ate the least. While people may not be willing to give up foods like red meat, even a small shift to eating less of it can make a difference.

Other studies document the problems caused by excessive sugar found in soft drinks, and simple carbohydrates like refined flour in most of the baked goods we eat. The rise in diabetes has a direct correlation to the increased use of sweeteners (like corn fructose) and the rise of obesity in America. All this has led me to create some simple guidelines I follow for energy, longevity and weight control. Here's how you can, too.

Avoid or limit:

- Saturated fats from dairy products, processed or red meat and the wrong oils (saturated or trans fats) found in most processed food

- Simple carbohydrates and non-naturally occurring

sugar found in pastries, desserts, soft drinks, white flour and most fruit juices

Get plenty of:

- Vegetables and whole fruits and nuts like almonds and walnuts

- Protein mainly from legumes (such as beans and lentils) and other plant products like soy. If more protein is needed, use plant-based protein powder supplements. For meat, choose fish such as wild-caught salmon or tuna followed by skinless chicken breast (which is lower in saturated fats than the dark meat)

- The right oils, especially those that have high levels of Omega 3

- Fiber from vegetables as well as grains including brown rice, oatmeal and whole wheat

- Antioxidants, such as those found in blueberries, açaí and pomegranate juice

- Water, while limiting juice consumption and cutting out soft drinks

It has been a slow journey as I have dropped some foods I loved and added healthy ones I can live with as an ongoing lifestyle choice. The journey continues: I have been most recently impacted by the book *The China Study: Startling Implications for Diet, Weight Loss and Long-Term Health* by T. Colin Campbell, PhD. It is the largest human study ever conducted on the connection between what we eat and a wide variety of diseases from heart to cancer to diabetes. The central finding is similar to previous studies – but with a twist. Animal fats are still the culprits, but the single major correlation between heart disease and diet is the percent of animal protein people eat. The less animal protein (in any form) we consume, the greater the impact on our health. Eating a primarily plant-based diet was found to be the answer to a healthier body in most all regards. (The film *Forks Over Knives* [www.forksoverknives.com] tells the story quite well.)

People generally start to look at their diet only when they gain weight and then they too often think in terms of short-term diets. The problem is diets don't work long term. The answer for anyone – whether overweight or not – lies in developing a consciousness about the right and wrong kinds of food to eat. That leads to selecting more of the right kinds of foods and avoiding the damaging ones. In time, the healthy foods become a preference and a way of life.

I do know that what I eat makes a difference. The cholesterol my doctor told me was a bit high back in the 70s (it was 220 then) more recently was measured at 150. I have very low "bad" LDL and triglycerides, and very high "good" HDL, as well as other favorable blood markers.

A good cardiovascular system contributes to energy, stamina, mental acuity and the ability to not be limited physically as we age. I entered my first sprint triathlons around 5 years ago and now compete in around six of them a year as one of very few in the "70 and over" age category. I believe that is possible because of my diet and my commitment to exercise. A healthy diet and regular exercise honors the body. It contributes to more time up the Mood Elevator, and less damage from stress.

Taking care of yourself and your body is the foundation for a longer fuller life and one in which you have the energy to do the things that are important to you.

So if you want to be as resilient and energetic as possible, take a look at what you eat and see if you can slowly move toward a diet that can be a healthier, long-term lifestyle way of eating.

Chapter Twelve

■ ■ ■ ■ ■ ■ ■ ■ ■ ■ ■ ■ ■ ■ ■ ■ ■

[energy levels: your guide to fitness]

Just as I suggested earlier in the book to "look to your feelings as your guide" to the Mood Elevator, I suggest you look to your "energy levels" as a guide to taking care of yourself. That requires developing the awareness to catch drops in your energy early. Once you know how to shift your energy back up, you can begin to develop an appreciation for healthy feelings – and a dislike for draining ones so they don't become "unhealthy normal."

high positive: **energetic, enthusiastic, inspired**

low positive: **reflective, grateful, loving**

high negative: **angry, hostile, self-righteous**

low negative: **worried, depressed, drained**

There are times when we have all of the positive and productive energy we need to face life. Then there are times when we are run down, overwhelmed and aren't so sure we have the energy to cope.

I have a special interest in managing my energy and taking care of myself. I am a 77-year-old man who has an 12-year-old as my youngest son. Logan is active in all kinds of sports and other activities, from basketball to skiing to surfing to the trampoline. He expects me to keep up – and I feel I owe it to him to be able to do so.

I also have a deep passion for the work Senn Delaney does to make a positive difference in the world by inspiring leaders to create thriving organizational cultures. That means helping people and teams operate at their best. I can do that work around the world with our clients only so long as I have the energy to do it.

Both my personal life and career purpose have led to my high level of interest in research on fitness and longevity and the best practices in energy management.

As I began to study and observe more about what it took to operate at my best, I developed a deep appreciation of the connection between being at my best physically, and being at my best personally and professionally. I came to value a fully present, calm yet engaged mind. My old hyper state became a "loud bell," one I disliked and learned ways to back away from.

Tony Schwartz (along with two other authors) has written a newer book entitled *Be Excellent at Anything: The Four Keys to Transforming the Way We Work and Live*. It is a continuation of his interest in managing energy as a part of his work as founder, president and CEO of The Energy Project.

I found two of the diagrams in Schwartz's book particularly relevant to taking care of yourself. "The Emotional Quadrants" presents many of the same levels as the Mood Elevator, especially as it relates to high-sustained performance in our "Stretch and Recover" model.

One of the quadrants, "The Performance Zone," includes energy states that drive high performance like optimistic, engaged and invigorated. Recovery takes place in energy states like peaceful, mellow and carefree – i.e., the "Renewal Zone."

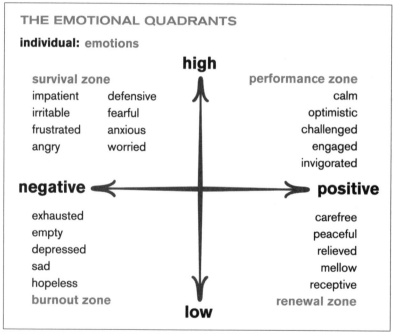

THE EMOTIONAL QUADRANTS

individual: emotions

high

survival zone   performance zone
impatient   defensive   calm
irritable   fearful   optimistic
frustrated   anxious   challenged
angry   worried   engaged
                                           invigorated

negative ⟵——————————⟶ **positive**

exhausted   carefree
empty   peaceful
depressed   relieved
sad   mellow
hopeless   receptive
burnout zone   **renewal zone**

low

Source: Be Excellent at Anything: The Four Keys to Transforming the Way We Work and Live. By Tony Schwartz. Used by permission.

Mood states that drain energy, such as impatient, irritated, angry and worried, are listed in the "Survival Zone." That leads to the "Burnout Zone," where we are exhausted, empty, depressed and sad.

The key learning element pointed out by Schwartz is that, "the optimal rhythmic movement in this dimension is between the positive energy we are feeling when we are operating at our best – The Performance Zone – and the Renewal Zone, where emotional recovery occurs."

Schwartz and his co-authors have organized many of the elements that play a roll in recovery and renewal in a second matrix they call "The Renewal Quadrants."

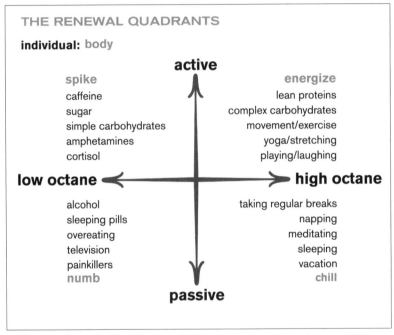

Source: Be Excellent at Anything: The Four Keys to Transforming the Way We Work and Live. By Tony Schwartz. Used by permission.

Things that help build our energy are found in the "Energize" quadrant. These include eating the right kinds of foods, getting exercise and engaging in social activities that lift the spirit.

The things that can renew us are found in the "Chill" quadrant. These are the things that physically restore us – like sleep and quiet time away from work.

Unhealthy escape mechanisms, like overeating and drinking alcohol, can be found in the "Numb" quadrant. While these items may provide temporary relief from stress and help relax us, they actually deplete our energy rather than renew it.

The things we too quickly (and routinely) turn to for a quick fix for our low energy can be found in the "Spike" quadrant. While caffeine, sugar and other uppers can give us a burst of energy, that peak is followed by a valley. The items that spike us also mask our true energy levels – making it less likely that we will deal with our need for renewal in a healthy way. The more items we can transfer from the Spike quadrant to the Energize quadrant, and from the Numb quadrant to the Chill quadrant, the better able we are to manage our energy in the long term.

Pay attention to your energy for the best ride on the Mood Elevator. Use not only your feelings as a guide, but your energy levels as well. Peak performers in all fields stretch and recover. You probably feel like you are already stretching – but how are you doing at recovery?

■■■■■■■■■■■■■■■■

[the second key: cultivating an attitude of gratitude]

"To speak gratitude is courteous and pleasant, to enact gratitude is generous and noble, but to live gratitude is to touch heaven."

– Johanna A. Gaertner

Taking care of yourself is one of the two most powerful things that are vital to shifting your set point on the Mood Elevator. The other is the cultivation of a specific state of mind. Since it is our thinking that creates our mood, the relevant question to ask is, *What state of mind or thought habit should I cultivate to best ride the Mood Elevator and be at my best?*

I recently watched a video that captured what that mindset is. It was called "The Power of Words." At the time that I viewed it on YouTube, almost 10 million people had also watched it. It is the story of a blind man sitting on a sidewalk with a coffee can for donations in front of him and a sign that said *"I am* blind, please help me." An occasional passerby would make a donation, but contributors were few and far between.

A woman passing by looks at his sign, thinks for a minute and then writes a new message on the reverse side of the sign.

Almost immediately, people walking by the blind man begin to stop, and the donations dramatically increase. He is both confused and amazed by the sudden and unexpected generosity of people passing by. When the woman returns later in the day, the blind man asks, *"What did you do with my sign?"* She replied, *"I wrote the same thing, just different words."* Then the sign is revealed. It says, *"It's a beautiful day and I can't see it."*

That little video evoked emotions in me, as I'm sure it did in many others. It was a poignant example of how we take too much of the wonder of life for granted, and in the rush of the day we lose our perspective. I believe that as people saw that new sign, it struck them how fortunate they were. The picture of the blind man begging on a beautiful day they could see and fully enjoy when he could not, touched a nerve that made them feel fortunate in comparison.

The mindset or thought habit we need to develop that most impacts our thinking (and therefore our experience of life) is perspective. But it's a particular form of perspective – a gratitude perspective.

> "Counting your blessings is more than a platitude; it is a pretty good way to maintain perspective."

The Top of the Mood Elevator

I have been asked often why gratitude is at the top of the Mood Elevator. It has been thoughtfully and intentionally placed there for many reasons.

Gratitude is what we might call an overriding emotion. If you think about it, it is almost impossible to be grateful and angry or depressed at the same time. There is a calmness and warmth that comes with gratitude that overrides sadness, impatience, irritation and anger.

Because gratitude is an emotion that connects us to a higher spirit, we are more purposeful and present and supportive of others when we are in that state of grace. Since it's more about others than it is about us, gratitude also overrides lower mood states like righteousness, envy and feelings of being victimized and powerless.

The reality is that we each have our own Mood Elevator – and what we have shown throughout these pages are simply composites of various forms that the elevator might take. Gratitude is near the top but not at the top for all people. A good case can be made that *wisdom* is the highest level because that is the level that represents the times we are more connected to universal intelligence. In moments like those, original thoughts occur as insights – and that can cause us to be at our best and highest self.

The case can also be made that love in the agape or unconditional form is at the top of the elevator. And it may well be. Gratitude is still my choice for the highest level because of the way it affects who we are and how we see life. When we focus on gratitude, we have a kind of perspective that impacts the way we see everything in life. It is almost axiomatic that when we lose our gratitude perspective, we engage in lower-quality thinking, which takes us down the Mood Elevator. Conversely, when we have perspective and can view our life and what it has to offer in all its totality, we stay up the Mood Elevator.

If you are reading this book and thinking about self-actualization (i.e., maximizing your potential and abilities) and not where your next meal is coming from, you already have a lot going for you. You are among a small percentage of people on the planet who are *not* living at a subsistence level. So many people have so much less than we do – not just in third world countries but closer to home.

I live near Pacific Coast Highway (PCH) in Southern California. I periodically see people pushing shopping carts containing all their worldly possessions down the highway. Compared to them we are blessed.

Yes, life does present its challenges. I wish I didn't have to be away from my family so much travelling to carry out the work of Senn Delaney. I wish I hadn't had to deal with loss of loved ones, including my parents and sister. But compared to that homeless person with their shopping cart, I'm a blessed man – and even the homeless are fortunate to be in Southern California where it's not too cold.

The way we can choose to view life and the impact that has on us can be seen symbolically in the illustration on the next page. If 100% represents the ideal, and zero represents how bad it could be, we are all closer to the top than the bottom.

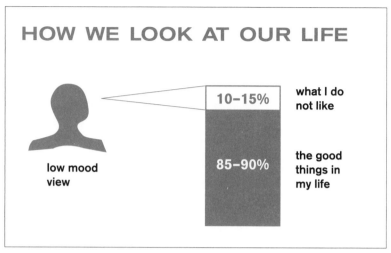

HOW WE LOOK AT OUR LIFE

10–15%	what I do not like
85–90%	the good things in my life

low mood view

If we choose to focus our thoughts on what we don't have or what we don't like (as in the diagram above), we won't feel good about life. We will be down the Mood Elevator as long as those thoughts dominate. Almost all the states toward the bottom of the Mood Elevator, including depression, represent times we have lost perspective. There may be many good things in our life, but without perspective in those moments of despair, the things we don't like or don't want become over-whelming and can consume us.

If we can fully appreciate all we have (as in the illustration that follows) and keep what we don't have in perspective, we experience life as full, rich and rewarding.

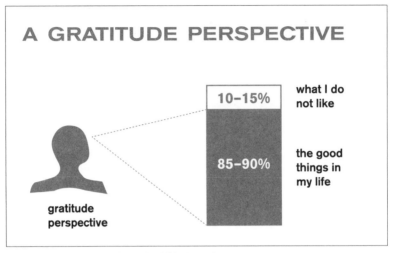

A GRATITUDE PERSPECTIVE

| 10–15% | what I do not like |
| 85–90% | the good things in my life |

gratitude perspective

No matter what is going on, at the very least we can be grateful for the miracle of life itself. Just to have consciousness and be able to experience the world around us is a gift. The ability to see a beautiful day is a gift we have that the blind man in the YouTube video didn't. Most people walking by him weren't noticing the gift of sight until they saw his sign saying, "It's a beautiful day and I can't see it." We lose sight of what life offers and can become consumed by what we don't have versus what we do.

A gratitude perspective is simply stepping back and looking at all we have. Being and feeling grateful is a great way to over- come negativity in our life. Bringing something to mind that you are grateful for can snap you out of a bad mood – and back up the Mood Elevator.

The Benefits of Gratitude

In her book, *Thank You Power*, Deborah Norville listed the many benefits people received by following a regular practice of keeping in touch with what they were grateful for in their lives:

PEOPLE WHO PRACTICE GRATITUDE

- felt better about their lives as a whole
- were more optimistic
- were more energetic
- were more enthusiastic
- were more determined
- were more interested
- were more joyful
- felt stronger about handling challenges

Book Excerpt ©2007 *Thank You Power*. Author Deborah Norville. Used with permission. Page 24

Stephen Post, PhD, is a researcher and professor of bioethics at Case Western Reserve University's School of Medicine in Cleveland. Post created a research group dedicated to testing and measuring the effects of love and other positive, caring emotions. His studies have shown that love-related qualities like gratitude actually make us physically healthier. Here are five discoveries Post shares about the power of gratitude:

1. Defends

Just 15 minutes a day focusing on the things you are grateful for will significantly increase your body's natural antibodies.

2. Sharpens

Naturally grateful people are more focused mentally, and are measurably less vulnerable to clinical depression.

3. Calms

A grateful state of mind induces a physiological state called resonance that is associated with healthier blood pressure and heart rate.

4. Strengthens

Caring for others is draining. But grateful caregivers are healthier and more capable than less grateful ones.

5. Heals

Recipients of donated organs who have the most grateful attitudes heal faster.

Research by University of California, Davis, psychology professor Robert A. Emmons, PhD, indicates that *"grateful people take better care of themselves and engage in more protective health behaviors like regular exercise, a healthy diet (and) regular physical examinations."* His research finds that grateful people tend to be more optimistic – a characteristic that boosts the immune system.

A fascinating and illuminating research project entitled "Dimensions and Perspectives of Gratitude" (sponsored by the John Templeton Foundation and led by Emmons) found that those people who kept gratitude journals received many benefits. They exercised more regularly, reported fewer physical symptoms, felt better about their lives overall, were more optimistic when facing life's challenges and made better progress towards work or life goals.

Grateful people also report higher levels of positive emotions, life satisfaction, vitality, optimism and lower levels of depression and stress. The attitude of gratitude enhanced high-mood states, but did not interfere with people's ability to face reality about the negative aspects of life.

Emmons found that while gratitude does not require religious faith, faith enhances the ability to be grateful. Grateful people are more likely to have faith in something beyond themselves, a belief in a connectedness of all life and a feeling of responsibility toward others.

Harvard and Stanford graduate Sonja Lyubomirsky, PhD, professor of psychology at the University of California, Riverside, focused on the scientific "how" of gratitude in her book, *The How of Happiness: A New Approach to Getting the Life You Want.*

Rather than theories or philosophies, Lyubomirsky extensively researched the practices that elevated one's spirits. She found that the kinds of activities that help raise your mood or set point for happiness include:

- expressing gratitude
- cultivating optimism
- avoiding social comparisons
- performing acts of kindness
- nurturing relationships
- forgiving others
- pursuing "flow" experiences
- savoring life's pleasures
- pursuing spiritual growth
- exercising and other good health practices

The bottom line: If you want to be happier, forget the myth that achievements or acquisitions will bring happiness; instead, focus on the kinds of activities you engage in and the thoughts you feed.

Gratitude and Emotional Intelligence

A gratitude perspective also helps us create more success with less stress because it boosts our emotional intelligence. When we have perspective, particularly a gratitude perspective, we have access to other higher mood states such as wisdom, insight, resourcefulness, hope and optimism. All these create better relationships as well as more success in life. Gratitude perspective provides the direct path to higher emotional intelligence: offering higher self-awareness of our state of mind moment to moment and the impact we are having on others. This also contributes to a more fulfilling and successful life.

The Role of a Quiet Mind

All of the higher levels of the Mood Elevator are accompanied by a quieter mind and the lower levels by a more hectic mind. Gratitude is no different. It occurs when we slow down and are fully present in the moment. Gratitude is difficult (if not impossible) to access with a very busy mind. That's why the feeling of gratitude is often connected with prayer or meditation, both of which quiet the mind and open the door to feelings like gratitude.

Learning to access gratitude is a very personal thing. Just like learning to better ride the Mood Elevator, you need to be self-taught through trial and error. It is like learning to ride a two-wheel bicycle. Someone can explain it to you, but you have to get the feel for it yourself.

There are several practices that contribute to an ongoing mindset of gratitude. Books such as Deborah Norville's *Thank You Power* suggest quiet journaling on what we are grateful for, or simply setting aside some reflective time to make the connection.

I find the following things helpful in maintaining an attitude of gratitude:

> **If you lead a hectic life and have a very busy mind, find ways to fit in quieter reflective time. I take the first few minutes when I wake up to use the breathing techniques discussed in Chapter 11 to be still. I then spend just a few minutes thinking about what I appreciate in my life, and how and why I want to be at my best that day for the benefit of all. I have a similar routine at night to quiet my mind before going off to sleep.**

I am touched by things throughout my day that remind me to be grateful. The trick is to stop yourself, take a breath and let the moment register so you truly "get it" and don't blow by it. It can be as simple as noticing a sunset or a beautiful morning. It might be something a child, friend or loved one does that has nothing to do with you, but makes you feel proud or apprecia-tive of having them in your life.

For me, it can be any expression of love from any of my five children. That can come in the form of a hug, a heartfelt "I love you, Dad" or notes, texts or emails I periodicity get. It causes me to stop and acknowledge to myself how fortunate I am.

There are numerous rituals that can help too. We've mentioned both journals and reflective time. For many years, my family has had a ritual at Thanksgiving where we take time between dinner and dessert to focus on what we are grateful for. This tradition probably happens in many households: One by one, each person talks about what they are most grateful for. We rarely get through it without some tears of gratitude.

My family and I decided that this ritual should be part of our daily lives, not just on Thanksgiving. So we created a year-round version of it. Whenever two or more family members are together for a meal, in addition to saying a simple grace, we added something we call a "high/low" game. Each person takes a turn and shares two things that they feel really good about from that day or week – the "high." They also share one thing that didn't go as well (the "low"). It creates a spirit of gratitude and personal connectedness and a chance to not only be real with each other, but supportive if there are challenges.

We also occasionally devote a dinner to "what I appreciate about you." We each get to share one thing we appreciate about another family member. It can be something specific they did or something about who they are.

Appreciation and Gratitude

Gratitude is an express button on the Mood Elevator. It turns out there is a second express button – it is sincere, genuine appreciation. It has been said that we pass along only one in 30 good thoughts that we have about others. Making it a practice to catch others doing things right – and generously sharing that appreciation – really lifts the spirits of others and ourselves.

In an interesting way, appreciation also connects us to gratitude. When I share with my wife, Bernadette, what a great mother she is and why, I feel grateful for the role she plays in our family and in my life. When I acknowledge my son Logan for his dedication in school or how thoughtful or loving he has been that week, I feel proud and grateful that he is my son.

Gratitude Perspective and Adversity

A gratitude perspective can also come from deep adversity. Many people gain a new appreciation for just being alive after a life-threatening event. My sister-in-law, Sybil, has been much more lighthearted and more grateful for the little things in life since she successfully fought her battle with breast cancer. She values the gift of life she regained; compared to what she went through, everything else is "the small stuff."

It is too bad that it takes a heart attack, near-death experience or some other major life adversity to put life in perspective. We all get so caught up in what we think is important that we often lose touch with what really is important. We lose our gratitude perspective.

A gratitude perspective in the face of adversity can empower us to deal with major setbacks in life. That's because anything that can take us to the top half of the Mood Elevator can help us operate at our best. That allows us to find solutions.

I needed to be at my best when I simultaneously faced three major life challenges in the year 2000. It happened right at the end of the dot-com boom, when many consulting firms were merging to get greater scale and added capabilities. Senn Delaney merged with a larger firm in a stock swap; unfortunately, that firm and the stock collapsed almost immediately. With it went the value in the firm I had built over a period of 25 years – as well as loss of control of the company.

Because Senn Delaney was still doing well, our resources were being drained to fund the larger organization. We concluded we had to find a way to buy our firm back, and knew it would be difficult – and a major battle.

Just as we began to take that challenge on, I was diagnosed with a cystic acoustic neuroma, a fast-growing tumor of the nerve that connects the ear to the brain. Since the tumor sat right on the 7th nerve (and in fact was attached to it), I was told one slip in the operating room and the left side of my face – including my mouth and eye lid – would be paralyzed; not a great prospect for a guy who makes his living in part by talking to groups.

As I was trying to absorb those two major blows, Bernadette came home from the doctor and announced she was pregnant. This was something we had wanted and hoped and prayed for, but hadn't expected since she was in her 50s and I was in my 60s. It was a triple hit: a major financial setback that wiped out much of my net worth, a brain tumor that was rapidly paralyzing one side of my face and a child on the way. It had been easy to be grateful when everything was going well, but how would I do when everything was not?

I decided this would be a great test of my understanding of the principles I had been teaching. I knew that being down the Mood Elevator with low emotional intelligence would *not* give me the wisdom or mindset to best address these challenges. Feeling worried, irrational, depressed and resentful were not a good base of operations in which to find solutions. So how would I get out of the lower floors of the Mood Elevator where I seemed so stuck?

Perspective, in particular a gratitude perspective, brought me back up the Mood Elevator. My thinking began shifting away from self-pity for my multiple woes to all that I could still appreciate in my life. It was a benign tumor and was operable; I wouldn't die from it. I had a loving and supportive family, and a child we had prayed for on the way. I had my health (aside from the tumor), and my work with leaders and organizations was fulfilling.

I began to participate in Bernadette's joy about our child and to count my blessings for all I did have.

From this higher-quality thinking I regained my wisdom. A team including Darin, one of my older sons, did the research to find the surgeon with the best track record in the world for my particular procedure, and somehow we got on his crowded calendar. Prayer groups with hundreds of people spontane-ously formed, and I went into a serious and risky operation with a serenity that was quite remarkable.

I found I had a new resolve and all the tools that a clearer, more hopeful mind provides. The operation to remove my brain tumor was a success. One of the downsides of the operation became another life lesson. The type of surgery that was best did eliminate hearing in my left ear and loss of inner ear balance. Oddly enough, this has actually helped make me a better listener because I now value being able to hear so highly. We creatively managed to find a way to buy the company back. And Bernadette gave birth to a beautiful, healthy son.

Facing my mortality led to a renewed commitment to physical fitness (and balance). It also gave me intense motivation to be alive and physically fit for my young son.

Once again, I found that the Mood Elevator — supported by a grateful state of mind — can help with almost any of the challenges we face. The lesson that came out of that whole experience was to have faith and hope that things can turn out when we are accountable for our thinking and operating at our best. But the biggest lesson for me was to be grateful for what I do have. I don't take my life for granted — and I also don't expect it to be perfect.

> "I have learned that some of the nicest people you'll ever meet are those who have suffered a traumatic event or loss. I admire them for their strength, but most especially for their life gratitude — a gift often taken for granted by the average person in society."
>
> – Sasha Azevedo

Unconditional Gratitude

You've probably heard of unconditional love; that's the kind of love a mother or father have for a child, or people with deep faith have in a higher power. It is a love that is in no way contingent.

While I don't know if it is fully attainable, an aspiration I hold is to continue on a path toward what could be called unconditional gratitude.

We normally associate gratitude with the "things" we are grateful for. "I am grateful because…" We have asked that question of thousands of people in our sessions, and the deeper things people are grateful for are very similar. The vast majority of folks list family or relationships and health as the two top things they are grateful for.

While it is true that thinking of loved ones or acknowledging other positive aspects of our lives can bring that momentary feeling of gratitude, unconditional gratitude is something else. It is a feeling of gratefulness for life itself, not for things or people. It is a form of gratitude for life as it is – and also as it is not.

Unconditional gratitude generally takes the form of a feeling – not a conscious thought, but a deep feeling of well-being, of being touched for no clear reason. It can be connected to a sense that we are part of something bigger and more important than ourselves. That is the feeling many people have in nature when they experience the splendor of a sunset, a beautiful forest, a rainbow, a tranquil lake or ocean waves breaking on a beach. For other people, gratitude has a spiritual quality to it – a knowing that there is a greater intelligence out there. From that perspective, it might be called a state of grace.

The commonality to all of this is a form of perspective that something much larger and grander than us exists – and our little problems are but a drop of water in an ocean.

When astronauts fly 150 to 250 miles above the earth, they get to view something that other human beings cannot. They see how thin and fragile the atmosphere is. They see how little land there is relative to the amount of water on earth. They can even see some of the destruction we have sown on vast areas like our rain forests. They see one tiny planet in a huge galaxy undivided by artificial political borders.

Astronauts all report coming back to earth with changes in their perspective. They feel as if they have come closer to seeing the bigger picture – something much bigger than them and much bigger than the petty issues and problems they may have complained about during their time in space.

One example of this attitude shift is that many astronauts come back as intense pacifists. They see the need for man to come together for the planet and set aside their differences. The ability to look at the cosmic "big picture" has a unique way of showing them that our problems are not that big. If we could all have that kind of epiphany, we could have more loving marriages and relationships, and far less conflict in the world.

I have so much to be grateful for. I believe and often tell others that I am a blessed man. But most people, including myself, only visit the unconditional gratitude level on the Mood Elevator periodically – we don't live there. But just knowing that gratitude is there, that it is accessible and knowing what it feels like is a great touchstone.

Whatever challenges you are facing in your life, know that there are even more things to be grateful for if you stop and count your blessings. Find your own ways to appreciate the life you have; that will contribute to what you achieve – and to the quality of the life you live.

part three

■■■■■■■■■■■■■■■■■

[change your thinking, change your mood]

"The greatest discovery of my generation is that human beings can alter their lives by altering their attitudes of mind."

– William James

Since it is our thinking that creates our feelings and our moods, it follows that if we could change our thinking, we could change our moods. It is not easy and often not possible to redirect our thinking, but there is one approach that can work.

The technique is called a *pattern interrupt*. It is simply a way to let go of one train of thought and switch to another.

Here is what it could look like in our everyday life. We are in a low mood, concerned about something that happened during the day. We may be obsessing about it and building our story. The phone rings; a good friend calls to say they have tickets to an event we have really wanted to attend and invites us. We begin to talk about how great it will be to go. Our mood shifts immediately because our thinking has shifted. It's a pattern interrupt. It can take dozens of different forms, and each person needs to discover what works for them.

"When patterns are broken, new worlds emerge."

– Tuli Kupferberg

When our 12-year-old son Logan gets really upset, bothered or angry, he lets my wife and I know it won't be productive if we try to talk to him when he is in the grip of his lower mood state.

He has created his own system to deal with it, and it works very effectively. He goes into his room, shuts the door and engages in activities he really enjoys. He picks things he can get lost in and which distract him from his lower-level thinking. That is usually something on his iPad®, Wii®, computer or television. It may be watching a favorite program or playing a game that takes his full concentration. Before long, he comes out of his room and is the loving, lighthearted son we know.

I heard Logan explain his process to his Sunday school class. "When I get real grumpy like that, it's not really me," he said. "I'm afraid I will say things I really don't mean, so I don't want to be around people. When I feel I'm myself again, I come back out and join the family." For Logan, his games are his pattern interrupt.

A good night's sleep is a healthy pattern interrupt. After a long day, the world looks overwhelming, people are irritating and answers aren't evident. We get a good night's sleep and though the circumstances haven't changed, our world looks better. That is because our thinking in the morning is different than what it was that night.

For me, exercise creates a mood lift. Running produces endorphins that create a natural high, this much we know, but it is more than that. The rhythmic pace, the music I listen to — it all clears my busy mind and quiets me down. My thinking shifts so my mood shifts. I may be tired and feeling low when I roll out of bed, but by the end of my run I am usually inspired, full of good ideas and ready to face my day. A good walk or any form of exercise can do the same thing. Just going out into sunlight and walking a few minutes can shift our thinking and our mood.

Exercise also brings with it an intake of oxygen and deeper breathing. Breathing in and of itself can be a "mini" pattern interrupt. The technique described in Chapter 11 of stopping to take a breath or two can calm you down. The commonality to meditation, prayer, exercise and deep breathing is that all of them quiet the mind.

Moods are contagious. Studies have shown that if you put a person with a low mood state into a group or a meeting, the tone of the whole group goes down. Conversely, if you put a person in a high mood state in a room, that higher mood state is also contagious. Whenever I get a bit weary and over-whelmed on long road trips for client work I call my wife, Bernadette. She will usually share something great that one of the kids has done. She will listen as I talk about my day and I can feel my spirits rising. I'm catching her higher mood. Bernadette is my "pattern interrupt" when I am in a low mood state.

While it is not good to generalize or categorize, I admit I tend to view people in my life as energy "pumps" or energy "drains." If I want an uplift, I will connect with someone who is already where I want to be on the Mood Elevator. That quality is something we select and hire to at Senn Delaney. If you ever meet anyone in our firm in any position or any office around the world, you will feel that positive energy right away. Spending time with people in your life who can raise your spirits can be a pattern interrupt – and an automatic mood shifter.

Self-talk can also make a difference in managing moods. I have used self-talk as a pattern interrupt to shift my worry habit. I first learned to recognize the onset of worry by the feeling – and by the fact that the thoughts went around and around in my head (my "mental eddies"). As soon as I noticed my spinning thinking, I would say to myself in a lighthearted, almost kidding kind of way, "There you go again!" or "Don't go there." Awareness and gentle reminders can catch a mood before it has a chance to take hold.

Focusing on others and higher purpose as a pattern interrupt

Nothing calls to our higher selves (and higher-quality thinking) more than a focus on a higher purpose or noble cause. It gets us out of our thoughts about ourselves and moves us into thinking about others and their needs.

Your purpose doesn't have to be a grand one. It just needs to be about something greater than you – something that makes a difference. It can be as simple as:

- Listening to a friend in need

- Contributing time or money to a worthy cause

- Committing to live a spiritual life and model those principles

- Coaching or being a team mom or dad for a kid's team

- Joining a run/walk for a worthy cause

- Helping someone who needs assistance

- Being an attentive and present parent, caring for and teaching values to your child

We raise our spirits and shift our mood whenever we get past ourselves and do something for others. It's a wonderful, self-reinforcing cycle. When we do for others, we stop being so concerned about ourselves and are more inclined to stay up the Mood Elevator. When we are on the higher floors, we are more purposeful and do more for others. It doesn't have to be a grand purpose; it can be the simple day-to-day acts of being there for someone else or contributing to something beyond you.

"Everyone I know who is happy is working at something they consider important."

– Abraham Maslow

The list of possible pattern interrupts is endless. Taking a walk, exercising, listening to music, helping a friend or child, reading a book, volunteering for a cause, taking a shower or bath, getting a massage, taking a nap, going shopping, stopping to watch a sunset – all these pattern interrupts can shift your thinking to a better place on the Mood Elevator.

I urge you to find the things that work best for you. One caveat: *They won't always work.* Sometimes we just get stuck. Which raises the question: What makes it so difficult to get out of a pattern of low mood states and what do we do if we are really stuck?

Here is the challenge we face. First, our thinking always makes sense to us in the moment (even if it doesn't really make sense); it is compelling and seems real. Second, we feel justified when we are facing a real problem or challenge, so we think we have a "right" to feel the way we do. Third, it is a part of life to ride the Mood Elevator up and down, and sometimes – for no apparent reason – we are down.

So if your preferred pattern interrupt (or a good night's sleep or exercise) doesn't make a dent in how you are feeling, the best thing to do is to treat the low mood state like bad weather. Get through it doing as little damage as you can to yourself and to others. When all that fails it is often best to not fight it but just surrender to being human. Know that, like the dark clouds in the sky, your low mood will pass and you will feel better again. It has happened before and will happen again.

The next page shows some pattern interrupts you may want to try the next time you find yourself in a low mood state. Remember:

"Change your thoughts and you change your world."

– Norman Vincent Peale

TRY PATTERN INTERRUPTS

- take a deep breath; relax
- use a word clue such as:

  "don't go there"

  "there I go again"

  "it will look different later"

- help someone else or a cause
- hold your thinking more lightly
- take a walk or a stretch break
- switch to an activity you like
- talk to someone who raises your spirit
- get some perspective; count your blessings
- know that, like the weather, this too shall pass

Chapter Fifteen

■ ■ ■ ■ ■ ■ ■ ■ ■ ■ ■ ■ ■ ■ ■ ■ ■

[separate realities: your world is not my world]

"It would probably astound each of us beyond measure to be let into our neighbor's mind and to find how different the scenery was there from that of our own."

– William James

A lack of understanding of separate realities is the root of most arguments, unsatisfactory relationships, many divorces, political battles and even wars. An understanding of separate realities makes great relationships and marriages, creates healthy, respectful dialogue and prevents us from making assumptions that take our thinking and feelings down the Mood Elevator.

The notion is simple. Two different people rarely have the exact same thoughts about any topic. Therefore, they live in "separate realities." To my wife, *The Real Housewives of Orange County* is an interesting television show; it's entertaining and helps her appreciate what a great relationship we have in contrast to those dysfunctional ones. I, on the other hand, can't understand why anyone would watch it, as I see no redeeming qualities.

In television viewing – and in far more important matters

such as child rearing – my wife and I each have our own point of view. To the degree that I am certain my thinking is right and my wife's is wrong, not just different, we have challenges. It is not always easy as my wife and I have strong filters based on historic thought habits that come from parental influences, as well as the nature of our up-bringing, religious education and life experiences. These differences in how we see situations can get in the way of our relationship if we let them.

Fortunately, we both understand that what we have is our "point of view," which we each need to respect and listen to. We also know each of us has blind spots that the other sees.

The picture below helps illustrate this concept. Can you see a face – a man with a big nose looking to your left?

Now what if I told you that this is actually a picture of a woman holding a baby? His nose is actually her hair and she may have on sunglasses. The baby is to your far right.

Most people see one or the other first and without the clues I gave, don't notice the other possibility. It happens to us almost everyday. Have you ever driven by something for years and then one day noticed it was there? Have you ever been absolutely sure something was one way, only to find out it was another? Have you ever sworn that someone said something, but they were certain that they didn't? Have you ever been sure you put the car keys one place and found them in another?

The mind is an amazing thing and life does play tricks on us. Both the man's face and the woman and the baby are apparent in the picture. You just happened to see one first and probably didn't notice the other right away. This happens hundreds of times in our daily lives. We all have selective perception: Based on our personal biases, past experience and how things are presented, we catch one part of the picture but miss others. Have you ever been absolutely sure something was one way, only to find out it was another? Have you ever sworn that someone said something, but they were certain that they didn't? Have you ever been sure you put the car keys one place and found them in another?

That is why two people can look at the same thing but see it differently. A lot of arguments could be avoided if we could just remember that things are not always what or how they appear to us, and that others are probably seeing it differently. The bottom line is our relationships and our moods suffer to the degree we lack humility and feel self-righteous about how we see things.

One of the saddest examples of an incorrect but righteous point of view is the surprisingly large number of people falsely convicted of crimes due to eyewitnesses. In recent years, thousands of convicted felons have been let out of prison based on irrefutable DNA testing. Some of these men and women have spent decades wrongly incarcerated. The majority of those released were convicted based on "certain" eyewitness account testimony.

In one case, enough contradictory evidence surfaced that a convicted felon was given a retrial some 10 years after incarceration. The eyewitnesses showed up at the courthouse to once again swear on the bible that there was absolutely no doubt in their mind that this person was the criminal. More years passed, DNA testing became available and evidence finally proved that someone else had committed the crime. That someone else was already in jail – and confessed when confronted with the evidence.

Recently, the police chief of Los Angeles announced with utmost certainty and conviction that the police department had caught the man who viscously attacked a San Francisco Giants fan after a Dodgers baseball game, putting the fan in a coma – and incensing a city. The arrest was based on (you guessed it) eyewitness identification. A few weeks later, the alleged assailant was released after he proved he had been elsewhere, and the real perpetrators of the assault were finally caught. The police chief, who had been so publicly certain, was forced to apologize.

Being too sure of how you see things and thus being too judgmental and self-righteous has lots of downsides. If the judgment level on the Mood Elevator becomes your "unhealthy normal," your experience of life will suffer. You will argue more, be more irritated and bothered and be more defensive and angry more often. Your relationships will suffer as your lack of understanding of separate realities and points of view creates more conflict than is necessary with people in your personal life and in your career.

You also are likely to develop a fixed vs. growth (i.e., learning) mindset. Since you are the expert – and so certain of how things are – you will be less open to considering other ideas, options and ways of seeing things.

How can you use the concept of separate realities to have a growth mindset? How can you have better relationships and higher-quality thinking? First, cultivate a curious mindset. When you encounter people and things you don't agree with, go to curiosity on the Mood Elevator not to judgment. Ask yourself "What is their thinking? Why do they see it differently?"

Try not to see it as your truth but your point of view – how it appears to you. Accept that there are almost always two sides to a story, more than one answer to a question and more than one solution to a problem. Be open to the input of others and be less certain or righteous when dealing with people who see things differently. Just say to yourself, "That might be a blind spot of mine. I better listen some more for what I might have missed or failed to consider."

Second, change your language to be less dogmatic and certain. Communicate more from a "point of view" rather than an absolute knowing. Here are a few useful qualifiers that give recognition to these principles and provide you with a better way in which to rephrase statements:

"It appears to me …"

"The way I see it …"

"From my point of view …"

"I think …" (versus "I know")

"If I'm not mistaken …"

Finally, as with all other pointers in this book, use your feelings as your guide. There is a feeling of intensity that goes hand-in-hand with certainty, judgment, self-righteousness and impatience with others. Become acquainted with these feelings of intensity and learn to recognize them when they pop up. They are signs you have stopped listening and learning – and are shutting off people and possibilities. Instead, look for the feeling of curiosity, of understanding, of patience. Sit back a moment, take a deep breath and, as Steven Covey so wisely put it, "Seek to understand before being understood."

Chapter Sixteen

■ ■ ■ ■ ■ ■ ■ ■ ■ ■ ■ ■ ■ ■ ■ ■

[seeing their innocence]

"You can work miracles by having faith in others. By choosing to think and believe the best about people, you are able to bring out the best in them."

– Bob Moawad

All too often we attribute motives to the way others deal with us, and in all too many cases our assumptions are wrong. Have you ever gotten mad at someone for something and then found out they didn't do it? Have you ever been sure someone deliberately undermined you, only to find that wasn't his or her intention at all? We have all had that happen to us in large and small ways.

It happened to me while I was traveling a few years ago. Though I live in Orange County, California, I often fly out of Los Angeles International Airport (LAX), some 30 miles north. There is an Orange County edition of the *Los Angeles Times* and on the day I was traveling, there was a local article of great interest to me based on the headline I saw. I had phone calls lined up right until flight time, and was really looking forward to getting settled in my seat and reading the article.

Once aboard, I set the paper on my aisle seat, and then looked around before finding an open space in the overhead bin for my carry-on bag. When I went to sit down, my paper was no longer on my seat – and the guy next to me in the window seat was reading the Orange County section. I immediately dropped my mood down to irritated and bothered – but then caught myself before dropping into angry or righteous. I took a breath and said to myself, *it's no big deal. It's not worth sweating the small stuff.* Then I went to sit down. As I did, I saw that my newspaper had fallen on the floor and the man next to me was reading his own copy of the newspaper. He turned out to be a great guy, and we talked about the article and other local news.

While my newspaper story is a small, humorous example, couples have divorced and countries have gone to war over assumed motives. Sometimes they *did* do it, but more often than not it was inadvertent, a misunderstanding, faulty or low-mood thinking that caused them to do it.

> They didn't do it.

My assumption of guilt toward my traveling mate almost took me down the Mood Elevator. How often do you get mad at someone for something they didn't do? It can be as simple as, "No! You took the car keys," only to find them in your pocket or purse. How may minor fights do we have with loved ones about imagined things they didn't do?

I heard a story once about a man who loved nature and was into conservation and preservation of our natural resources. As he was pulling into a campground in Yosemite National Park, he noticed a woman drop a bag of garbage on the ground – right next to the trash can.

He jumped from his car and ran over to share his irritation. Only then did he notice her red and white cane. He realized the woman was blind and had proudly (and with some difficulty) found the trash can but missed on the drop. She had placed her trash on the ground without realizing it. That clearly was not her intention.

They didn't mean to do it.

Well-intentioned people often do things inadvertently. We change lanes on the freeway and cut someone off because we didn't realize they were as close as they were. They may be swearing at us, or fighting off road rage, or saying to themselves that we were irresponsible. Or they may shrug it off because they realize they have done the same thing themselves. Stuff happens, and we react. We can't always control the events, but we *can* influence our reactions – because they take place in our thinking.

They got caught up in a low mood.

All of us have said things we wish we hadn't when we were caught up in low-quality thinking. We may even have believed what we said was justified in the moment. But when our higher-quality thinking returned, we realized what we were thinking was an over-reaction, inappropriate or out of bounds.

People lose their emotional intelligence in the low-mood states. They become socially inept, inappropriate and oblivious to the impact they are having on others. Smart people can inadvertently do very dumb things. The question for us is, can we have the wisdom to see that it is their mood talking – or do we take it personally?

I had an interesting experience with this while traveling recently. My flight was delayed, and I arrived at my hotel quite late at night. I was greeted by one of the least friendly, most surly desk clerks I have ever encountered. I felt like my being there was a real imposition on him; it was a burden to check me in. Initially he wasn't sure he had my reservation at all (which of course he found); then he complained about the weather, and the city, and having to work late. None of which I had an interest in – I just wanted to check in and go to my room.

It would have been easy for me to drop down to the lower mood state of irritated and bothered and tell him, "Just do your job because it's your job," but instead, for some reason I'm not quite certain of, I went up a few levels on the Mood Elevator to compassion and gratitude.

I felt sorry for this man whose life seemed so grim; I felt a great deal of gratitude for my life compared to his – and for the understanding I had that allows me to enjoy it so much. That led me to sympathize with him about his tough day, and I responded by saying, "It must be hard; I'd hate to have to work this late."

Rather than escalate into a confrontation, his attitude improved and he wished me a successful visit in his city. Most importantly, the encounter didn't ruin my evening; instead, it provided another example of how commitment to living life in the higher states of the Mood Elevator can make your life better.

They just see it differently than we do.

People can, in fact, do things that are detrimental to us. They can make us wrong and shoot down our ideas. They can have different positions on everything from politics to religion to child rearing. It isn't necessarily about us; it's just that they see things differently than we do.

The biggest challenge early on in my second marriage was how to deal with my young children, who lived with us much of the time. I wanted it to be an ideal experience for them so that they wanted to be with me, and to know how much I wanted and loved them. That made me a soft touch as a dad – and too short on reasonable guidelines. My wife, Bernadette, loved them, too, but wanted to help me raise them to be responsible and capable kids who could take care of themselves and contribute to our home life.

So long as it was about me being right and her wrong, every suggestion she offered up pushed my button, and I took it personally. Only when we both better understood that we had different points of view on raising the kids were we able to blend our approaches, and it worked out well.

Understanding that, in most cases, our own self-truth is just our point of view allows us to have healthier relationships in life.

In a surprising number of families, blood relatives are estranged: siblings from siblings, parents from children. Things have been said and done in the past that people can't let go of, and separation ensues. Sometimes it's subtle – a cool or distant relationship – but sometimes people stop talking altogether.

At Senn Delaney, we have found a dynamic similar to the estranged family scenario in the corporate world – even on very senior teams of major organizations. A teammate once said or did something and it never got cleared up; the connection was broken. Trust was lost, and both parties (as well as the organization) suffered as a result.

Fresh Starts

After we have spent time with a corporate team going over the same concepts we are exploring in this book (and many more), we ask the group to consider what Senn Delaney calls a "fresh start." We explain that little can probably be done to fully rectify whatever history led to the friction or trust issues that have developed. What happened in the past now exists only in memory. The healthiest path is to let go of that history and judge one another on how they work together going forward with their new level of understanding.

We remind the team that since they all are signed up to fulfill the purpose of their organization, they need to assume positive intentions about each other in order to have a fresh start. They also need to accept the fact that they will see things differently based on their own points of view. When fresh starts like this are entered into in the right spirit and at the right time, it can revitalize relationships within the group.

The notion of a fresh start can play a powerful role in mending any relationship. We can't fix the past but we can forgive it and start anew. Some times that's the only way to rebuild a damaged relationship. It takes being able to see past assumed transgressions with some degree of innocence and then to move on.

It is useful to understand that our *assumptions* determine the intensity of our reactions to what other people say and do. It goes something like this:

- If we think it was spiteful and personal, we feel justified in outrage and revenge.

- If we think it was intentional, we feel justified in anger.

- If we think it was gross negligence or they just don't care, we feel justified in harsh judgment.

- If we think it was unintentional but they should have known better, we feel justified to be irritated and bothered.

- If we think they lacked information, are uninformed, and just did what made sense to them, we can be understanding and patient, and work towards a solution.

- If we accept that they were in a low mood state, we can handle the issue with grace, not personalize it, and wait for the right time to resolve it.

In each of these cases, the event or comment could be the same; the variable is the "spin" we put on it. Our assumptions can result in emotions covering the full range of the Mood Elevator, from outrage and vengeance to understanding and compassion. The choice is ours.

Forgiveness is a key

The hardest thing is when we do all we can to see innocence and *still* feel we were genuinely wronged. We just can't forgive. The person may or may not have apologized, but the incident stays in our thinking and impacts our mood – especially when around them or when reminded of them.

I was out running early one morning while on an East Coast business trip. I hadn't had my morning reflective time and felt I needed a few minutes of quiet before a busy day with a client. I also had something on my mind that was bothering me. Something someone had done that I couldn't seem to let go of. I saw an open door of a church; I looked inside and no one was there. It is not a church I attend but it was peaceful and quiet, with beautiful stained-glass windows.

As I sat down and began to relax, I looked up and saw a large statue of Jesus on the cross with the words "Forgive them for they know not what they do" etched below. Somehow those words struck me quite powerfully that day. Who was I to hang on to small slights and resentments? Regardless of your religious persuasion, the notion of forgiveness is a universal, centuries-old concept that can help us in our modern life.

We each can have our very own form of "Forgive them for they know not what they do":

- They didn't know how important it was to us.

- They didn't realize they hurt us.

- They saw it differently than we did through their own filters.

■ They had their own lower moods, and it was their low-quality thinking talking.

The notion of seeing innocence is based on an understanding of the role of thought. Each of us is doing what makes sense to us based on our thinking. It is rarely personal. It is unlikely that someone is out to get us or to do things designed to bother us. They are just doing what follows from their thinking.

That doesn't mean we should let people take advantage of us, use us or abuse us. But when we can see what they are doing in innocence and not take it as personally, we maintain our bearings. We have mental traction – and are in the best emotional position to deal with whatever it is with wisdom. This allows us to have a better quality of life and to be more effective in relationships.

There is a connection between "fresh starts" and "seeing innocence." In a fresh start, we forgive the past and move forward without the weight and clouded thinking of the past. It is easier to do that when we don't attribute motives to the past action but, rather, see them as a form of innocence.

When we assume motives and ill intention, and hold on to past grudges, we are the one who suffers. The other person may not even know we are bothered – or care – but it is *our* quality of life that is affected as we spend more time in the lower mood states.

Learning to see the innocence is a great way to spend more of your time up the Mood Elevator, at home and at work.

.

Chapter Seventeen

■ ■ ■ ■ ■ ■ ■ ■ ■ ■ ■ ■ ■ ■ ■ ■ ■

[living in mild preference: the anecdote for irritated and bothered]

One of the lower levels of the Mood Elevator that many people drop into quite easily is irritated and bothered. This drop is usually blamed on events, circumstances or people not being the way we think they should be. It happens in relationships, in families, in the workplace and as we go about normal activities in our day-to-day life. Traffic was heavier this morning, the light turned red just as we reached it, our loved one has a habit that irritates us, we don't get the appreciation we deserve at work or at home (the list goes on). Life happens the way it happens – but we let it dampen our spirit.

What is interesting is that given the same life circumstances, some people are very easily irritated and bothered, while others can shrug it off and let it go. Some can quickly drop to irritated and then down to anger, while others are simply amused by how life plays out. Some get off the Mood Elevator and occupy the irritated level; others just pass by that floor occasionally.

There is a popular book you may have read that addresses this topic. It is called *Don't Sweat the Small Stuff...* by Richard

Carlson, PhD. The fact it became a best seller suggests to me that this is a common life condition most people face.

What's the difference between those people who don't seem to sweat the small stuff and others who are in a frequent state of bother? The answer: There is a distinct and definable difference in attitude towards life between those who are easily bothered and those who are not.

Those that are more easily bothered seem to have *a stronger need to have things be a given way*. People who get upset easily have more deep-seated beliefs about how people are supposed to be or behave, as well as stronger beliefs about how life is supposed to unfold. They may have higher standards, be more locked into "principles" as they define them and are probably more uncompromising.

If they can be discerning in where to apply those standards, and stick to them when that is appropriate, their philosophy may serve them well. However, if their higher standards become an unconscious habit used on big issues as well as small issues, they will spend a lot of unnecessary time at the irritated and bothered levels of the Mood Elevator. This will negatively impact their relationships and the quality of their lives.

Living in Mild Preference

People who spend less time in those lower mood levels seem to live in a world that could be called "mild preference." They are much more mindful and aware of when to put a stake in the ground. They, too, may have similar high standards and guiding principles – but they are more thoughtful in terms of when it matters.

Should we have Mexican or Italian food for dinner doesn't need to turn into WWIII. Traffic lights aren't programmed to stop just because we are in a hurry. Just because we don't agree with something someone says doesn't mean we need to go to battle over it. It is not a right or a wrong, it's just their point of view.

There may be a few critical issues in our lives that are non-negotiable, but on close examination most things in the scheme of life qualify as small stuff that should drop into the category of mild preference. It is truly a case of learning not to sweat the small stuff. And all that is required is maintaining perspective.

Bernadette and I have a remarkably tranquil and loving relationship. Living in mild preference is one of several foundational understandings she and I share that makes our tranquility possible. Mild preference prevents classic couple bickering and fights over what to eat when we go out, what movies to see or who we are rooting for in everything from politics to reality shows such as *Survivor*. Compared to our loving family, that's all small stuff.

The experience of life is different in these two worlds – the less forgiving world of strong preferences, and the more forgiving world of mild preferences. One keeps you up the Mood Elevator – the other drops you down.

A Humor Perspective

In Chapter 13, we talked about the importance of a gratitude perspective in shifting our set point on the Mood Elevator. The other life perspective that can impact our mood is having a *humor perspective*. That's why "sense of humor" is also listed in the top half of the Mood Elevator. Mild preference and lightheartedness are connected. We are less apt to be as fixed and rigid in our opinions and our needs when we can see the humor in life.

The most successful airline in U.S. history lists humor as a key strategy. Southwest Airlines is a no-frills, no-first class seat airline that is still frequently rated highest in the customer experience. Southwest hires people who are lighthearted and enjoy amusing others. When airplanes are delayed or weather is bad, they keep people's spirits up by finding ways to make the delay a comedy, not a disaster. When talking about the kind of people they look to hire, Southwest's co-founder, Herb Kelleher, said:

> "Life is too short and too hard and too serious not to be humorous about it. We look for attitudes, people with a sense of humor, who don't take themselves too seriously."
>
> – Herb Kelleher

Staying up the Mood Elevator plays a role in the success and profitability of Southwest in two ways. The positive experience people have gives Southwest more loyal customers; and the healthy attitudes of employees help them operate "at their best." The teamwork and camaraderie Southwest employees have helps them service and load and unload an airplane faster than anyone else. They work together in doing it – and even get the passengers to help.

We can all learn a lesson from Herb about having a humor

perspective. When we are experiencing a crazy day and encountering challenge upon challenge, we can become grim – or we can take a deep breath, step back and be amused by the insanity around us. When life gets extreme and we feel overwhelmed, we can choose to laugh or to cry. It is often better to just laugh at the occasional absurdity of life as it plays out. Learning to visit the sense of humor level on the Mood Elevator more frequently helps raise our spirits, access our full wisdom and clearer thinking and bring us through it in a healthier and more productive way.

Take Your Thinking More Lightly

During "down" times, it is easy to become gripped by our lower-level thinking. And yet it is during such times that our thinking is the most *un*reliable. The paradox is that we actually take our faulty thinking too seriously just when we should discount it the most. Learning to get a little distance from our thoughts when our low mood is talking can dramatically improve the quality of our lives.

Lots of benefits come from cultivating the habit of holding your thinking more lightly. When you do so, you:

- Listen better
- Are more open to new ideas
- See more possibilities and solutions
- Remain more creative
- Are more hopeful
- Are caught down the Mood Elevator less often

Letting go of lower state thoughts and feeling is not always easy or possible. If we are irritated, then in our minds we have a justifiable reason to be irritated. If we are judgmental, than surely something is wrong with the person or situation we are annoyed with. It takes a different kind of awareness – and a willingness to be guided by our feelings (not our thinking) to avoid sliding down the elevator over even minor things.

Our feelings are always our guide and we can use them to practice living in milder preference. Here is a way to do that. When, for example, the feeling of judgment comes up, first pause and notice it so you can be in choice and not on autopilot. Next, decide if the situation is significant enough to react to or just a mild preference of yours that you can let go.

Similarly, if you are impatient or bothered, first notice the feeling – then make a choice about whether it is small stuff in the grander scheme of things that you can let go of, or something you should dwell on and surrender your energy to.

Even if you choose to deal with what triggered your judgment or bother, you will do so in a much more thoughtful way because of the slight delay to make the choice.

A Metaphor

One aspect of my frequent air travel serves as a wonderful metaphor for the difference between mild preference and more rigid thinking. I am on an airplane flying somewhere most weeks and I never check my luggage. I do this because I want to take the potential irritation of lost luggage and waiting for baggage out of my experience. That makes me a carry-on luggage guy.

I have a roller bag that I pull down the aisle to get to my seat (which is usually in the economy section) and put in the overhead bin. The challenge comes because some planes have narrower aisles than others. When that is the case, my roller bag keeps banging into one side and then the other as I walk down the aisle.

When deplaning, with others anxious to get off the plane behind me, I move fast – and that creates even more problems. The faster I try to go, the more the bag bounces off one armrest and rams into the other. Sometimes my bag flips over sideways and I end up dragging it.

Other airplane configurations have aisles that are just a couple of inches wider – not much, but just enough. On those flights I can smoothly and effortlessly move up and down the aisle without hitting any seats. Those few inches make all the difference in my traveling experience.

Life is like that. If our aisles are too narrow and our preferences too strong, life can be much harder. We keep bumping into thought patterns and feelings we could avoid. Instead, try opening up your aisles just a bit and see if the concept of mild preference can reduce how often you are feeling dogmatic, irritated, judgmental or bothered.

[healthy relationships]

Many of the concepts described in this book – from mild preference to separate realities to seeing innocence – can be used to create better relationships at work and more loving relationships at home. And when it comes to building relationships, nowhere is the Mood Elevator more helpful. That's because our connection to others and to the world is dependent on how well we manage the ride on the Mood Elevator.

When we are down, we feel all alone. We don't feel connected. We tend not to reach out to others or be as supportive of them.

When we are in the lower mood states, people bother us more easily. We are more judgmental of others and tend to assume motives in what they do and say. Irritation, bother, judgment and anger are not good places to come from in creating supportive, collaborative relationships.

But it's a different story altogether in the higher mood states, because a healthy state of mind and healthy relationships are related.

There is a notion in Eastern philosophy of keeping your karma clean. My simple interpretation of that: Go out of your way to make more friends and no enemies, and life will somehow go better.

In the business world, we often talk about the importance of collaboration and teamwork. All too many organizations have "we/they" issues, trust issues, lack of cooperation between different departments, strained relationships between the corporate office and the field organizations and other relationship dysfunctions.

Relationship issues exist in families. While there are many loving and supportive couples and families, there are also an amazing number of dysfunctional ones. There are brothers and sisters who don't forgive one another for minor slights, in-laws who are considered outlaws and couples that constantly bicker.

Those unhealthy relationships flourish when people are in the lower levels of the Mood Elevator. They say things that hurt their partners and do things that are inconsiderate because their thinking is unreliable.

People who have a high emotional intelligence (EQ) and are aware of their moods have better relationships. They manage the Mood Elevator better, get along with others better and create better networks that lead to better success in life.

Emotional intelligence is nothing more than being aware of your own state of mind – that is, where you are on the Mood Elevator – and the impact that is having on others and being able to adjust accordingly. Emotional intelligence also includes an awareness of where other people are in their own state of mind, where they are on their Mood Elevator and the ability to adjust to that as well.

The Key To Close Relationships

It is easy to see how relationships are tied to the Mood Elevator. Who wants to be around someone who spends too much time in the lower states like depressed, self-righteous, judgmental, bothered or angry?

On the other hand, isn't it energizing to be with people who are more often in the higher mood states, like hopeful, optimistic and understanding? Wouldn't you rather be with someone who had a sense of humor than someone who mostly was just irritable?

People who are critical and judgmental of others, who are unforgiving and who anger easily are not likely to build networks of supportive relationships. It is like they have a bank account but the currency called goodwill is overdrawn.

The healthier levels of the Mood Elevator that lead to good relationships in life include compassion, forgiveness, curiosity, understanding and sense of humor. People are also more likely to attract other people to them when they are more hopeful and optimistic.

In the higher mood states, people commit to a higher purpose such as family; in the lower states, it is "all about me." It is easy to see how concern for the greater good builds relationships at work and at home.

If we are concerned about and interested in others and are willing to play win-win in a more unselfish way, we develop those strong relationships. But if it is "all about me" and I view the world through a win-lose set of glasses, my relationships suffer.

A Mood Elevator depicting your closest relationship may have some slight variations from the one you might create for your life in general. The lower floors of a relationship Mood Elevator are likely to contain feelings like irritated, projecting motives, taking things personally, overly sensitive, defensive, righteous, angry and unforgiving.

The higher mood states in a healthy relationship with a partner or loved one in life would include patient, comfortable, understanding, compassionate, forgiving, caring, supportive, respectful and loving.

Relationships and Success in Life

Relationship skills are a foundation for a more successful and fulfilling life. Years ago, I read a small but interesting book entitled *The Luck Factor*. It described a series of theories on the concept of luck. The theory that resonated with me the most was that "lucky" people have a much wider and stronger network of supportive relationships. The example I recall is a woman who got the dream job she never expected would be offered. As they traced the job offer back, they found she had created a network of very supportive people who "showed up" as she sought the job. Her references were glowing; her reference letters strong, and (unbeknownst to her) there were people she knew who knew people within the organization who came forward in her support.

The concept of Six Degrees of Separation (the notion that

everyone on the planet is connected to everyone else by six links) – makes sense to me. We are all connected in one way or another. People who better manage their Mood Elevator have far more connections and support systems than those who don't. That is why their lives seem to work better.

In order to have good relationships, let your feelings be your guide. To do that, look for and cultivate feelings of understanding, compassion, love and warmth towards others. This is often hardest in those closest to us because they are often the ones who can most easily push our buttons.

It takes conscious awareness to assume best intentions (not motives) in loved ones and a willingness to forgive. Accepting the idiosyncrasies of others, particularly loved ones, and developing the compassion to forgive "the things they do to us" is the key to healthy, loving relationships.

Strive to see innocence in the humanness and imperfections of loved ones. It takes the ability to see a form of innocence in how they show up and what they do and say. Not innocence that they didn't do it (because they probably did). It is deeper than that. It is grasping the concept that everyone is doing the best they can in the moment because they are just doing what makes sense to them in their thinking.

This understanding depersonalizes the perceived wrongs (or flaws) in our loved ones. We don't take the insecure behavior or their quirks as personally. It also leaves us in a much better mental state with more wisdom and common sense to deal with them in a healthier and more loving way.

Most of us spend the majority of our lives in relationships

with parents, family, loved ones and co-workers. Understanding how to spend more time in the upper states of the relationship Mood Elevator – and how to get there – greatly improves our quality of life and that of those around us.

Chapter Nineteen

[why did that happen for me?]

"What if the trials of this life are your blessings in disguise?"

– Laura Story

iving life up the Mood Elevator is greatly dependent on how we react when we face adversity. Life happens – including seemingly bad things. It is what we make of those things in our thinking and the path we choose that determines the quality and the relevance of our life.

Some people bounce back even stronger after adversity and some don't. Marilyn Hamilton was one who came back stronger and more purposeful. Growing up as a young woman in Fresno, CA, Marilyn had it all: a loving family, good looks (she was a former beauty queen), an accomplished athlete in tennis, skiing and other sports and an adventurous spirit that eventually led her to teach school in Australia. But one fateful day in 1979, while hang-gliding in the mountains near her hometown in California, she neglected to correctly fasten her lynchpin to her harness. She crashed into the side of the mountain and woke up a paraplegic – paralyzed from the waist down.

"I realized I was in trouble when, at the rehab center, I tried to sit up and immediately fell to the side, like a rag doll," Marilyn remembers. Weeks of physical therapy followed. She found that even the best wheelchairs available were, as Marilyn called them, "steel dinosaurs."

"People looked at me with pity, like I was sick," Marilyn observed. "But I wasn't sick. I was the same Marilyn, just with a different mode of getting around in the world."

She decided to do something about it. So Marilyn and her hang-gliding buddies set up shop in a garage in Fresno, CA and designed an entirely new wheelchair – composed of the same aerodynamic materials used in hang-gliders. These chairs were lightweight, fast, very maneuverable and flexible, so the parts could be adjusted to fit the user's body and specific disability needs. They jazzed them up, painting them pink and purple and other vibrant colors. They even decorated Marilyn's new chair with rhinestones and named it, *The Quickie*. What they did was much bigger than giving Marilyn a fun, sexy chair that reflected her personality – they changed the world forever for people with disabilities.

Today, the Quickie brand is sold around the world, and one of Marilyn's original wheelchairs is showcased in the Smithsonian Institute in Washington, D.C. Marilyn has gone on to win numerous medals for wheelchair sports, including U.S. Open tennis tournaments and skiing competitions. She has been featured on network television shows, including *60 Minutes*, and has testified before Congress. She received the Minerva Award at Maria Shriver's Women's Conference in 2006, and is known the world over as a spokesperson for people with disabilities.

Marilyn once observed, "It is not what happens to you in life that molds you; rather, it is how you respond. My motto is, 'If you can't stand up, stand out.'" Marilyn is a wonderful example of the central them of this book – that life is what you make of it in your thinking.

> "Even those experiences that we deem calamitous can carry the seeds of a greater blessing. It is often in retrospect, however, that the benefit reveals itself. And whether or not it reveals itself, and how quickly it does so, is dependent upon only one thing: our own individual perspective."
>
> – Kim Nowak

A common and understandable way many people respond to an adverse event or circumstance is by asking, "Why did that happen to me?" This path of questioning leads to lower mood states marked by blame, judgment and even depression. Instead, try taking a somewhat counter-intuitive approach by asking, "Why did that happen *for* me?" This less-traveled path puts us higher up the Mood Elevator, prompting curiosity, resourcefulness and optimism.

Whether we approach adversity with an accountable stance or as a victim of circumstance determines how well we respond to things that happen to us. During difficult times, it is helpful to slow down and ask yourself, "What can I learn from this? How can I avoid this in the future?" Or even, "I wonder where this path might lead?" Stepping up and questioning how you might benefit from a bad situation engenders a sense of curiosity, which in turn helps sow the seeds of faith that no matter what happens, you will make the best of it – and everything will turn out okay.

"Things turn out best for people who make the best of the way things turn out."

– John Wooden, The Wizard of Westwood

I have studied a variety of religions in my life. UCLA's former basketball coach John Wooden's quote brings one of them to mind because of its unconventional approach to prayer. Instead of asking for a specific outcome when you pray, the teaching says that your prayer should be for the "right outcome."

In essence, the prayer is for the right path to be revealed – that we will have the wisdom to see, do and say the right things and choose the right path. Woven into this prayer is an assumption that we don't always know what's best for us, nor do we know for sure whether what's happening to us is bad or, in fact, something for our ultimate good that is disguised.

This message reminds me of an old Eastern tale about a farmer and his family. The farmer was dependent on his hard-working son, but when the son broke his leg, it was seen as a major disaster and threat to the family's livelihood and well-being. It was not until the Emperor's guards came to their village to round up all the able-bodied young men for a distant war (from which most would not return) that the son's temporary disability was then seen as a great gift.

Seemingly "bad" things can turn out to be good things. I know this from experience. There would be no Mood Elevator, no Senn Delaney culture-shaping firm, no Logan and Kendra (my two youngest children) and no Bernadette (my wife and soulmate) if I had not gone through what felt like the most difficult experience in my life.

It was the ending of my first marriage mentioned earlier. The last thing in the world I wanted at that time was for my marriage to be over. It was the most painful thing that had ever happened to me, and I could see no possible benefit and no bright future. As I looked back on the experience some years later, it became very clear that this event was something that had happened *for* me, not to me. It was, in fact, possibly the *best* thing that could have happened in my life. It ultimately led to a whole new direction in my career, a new life purpose, a deeper relationship with my children and a "second life" that I cherish so much today.

The break-up got my attention and caused me to reflect on what was really important and what my purpose on earth was. I became clear that my family was important and doing work that made a positive difference was my calling.

It was our three boys (Kevin, Darin and Jason, then ages 7, 5 and 3) that gave me perspective. I had taken them for granted. They were just "there." While I did spend time with them, it was more dutiful than deeply connected and whole-hearted. A renewal of my focus on what truly was important – my sons – first cleared my thinking.

I regained perspective. I became very clear that my children were what was truly important. My immediate purpose became about building a closer, more unconditionally loving relationship with them.

That whole process jolted me out of a world filled with distorted priorities, unconscious habits and "unhealthy normal." I began a journey to know myself and to discover deeper meaning in my life. I created a strong and loving bond with my three boys that holds just as strong today. Without the wake-up call, that wouldn't have happened. It was what it took to tune me in to the bigger picture and give me new perspective on life. It made me deeply grateful for my family and loved ones, and for the power of fresh starts.

The experience also caused me to challenge my beliefs and behaviors, and see more possibilities for myself as an evolving human being. It led me to question my purpose in life, change the direction of my professional career and as a result, ultimately to found Senn Delaney – a firm that embodies my true mission.

My process of self-discovery led me to a better understanding of myself (including what it takes to be a great life mate). And that led me to Bernadette and another round of children who are the joy of my life.

> "Every adversity, every failure, every heartache carries with it the seed of an equal or greater benefit."
>
> – Napolean Hill

Things that happen *to* us don't always turn out well, but taking the "why did it happen *for* me?" stance guarantees learning – and a far superior outcome than taking the victim path.

Once again, the Mood Elevator illustrates how an unconventional viewpoint of even bad events can lead you down a better path. You can take the low road of "why did it happen *to* me?" or the high road of "why it happened *for* me."

When I changed my thinking and took the more curious route of asking "why did this happen *for* me?" it led to deeper reflection and a greater appreciation for life.

Chapter Twenty

■■■■■■■■■■■■■■■

[faith, hope and optimism]

ike curious, there is another very special level on the Mood Elevator. It is useful for letting go of thoughts that generate irritation, bother, judgment and worry. It is a very life-enhancing concept – and one that creates more success with less stress. Here's how it works.

What if you knew at some level that no matter how serious something you were concerned about was, it would all work out OK?

What if you were feeling overwhelmed but knew somehow you would handle it?

What if a close friend or loved one did something that really bothered you – made you mad and feel distant – but you knew your love or friendship would prevail and you would be close again?

What if you were having a really down day but you were confident that "this too shall pass" and it would soon look better?

In each case, that hopeful thinking would make you less inclined to dwell on the negative thoughts. You would be less likely to catastrophize. It would be easier to drop the thoughts creating the low mood and be more hopeful and effective.

In each such situation you face, you probably would not have "the" answer to the challenge nor know exactly what to do to change it. So what is it you would have that would allow you to still handle these situations creatively with more ease and grace?

What you would have is faith – faith that there would be an answer, that you could handle it, that it would somehow work out. That faith would give you hope and that hope would give you wisdom. As you moved to higher levels on the Mood Elevator, your emotional intelligence would kick in with plenty of common sense, perhaps some useful insights and added wisdom.

One definition of faith is a strong or unshakable belief in something, without proof or evidence. It is confidence or trust in an outcome or in a person without fully knowing why or how. Faith and hope are often linked because faith gives one hope, and hope creates possibilities and healthier, more resourceful thinking.

My daughter, who is in the business school at University of Southern California, asked me the other day why she had to take a complex math course for which she could see no possible use in her career. I explained to her one of my theories of the purpose of college. Yes, it is to educate, but more than that it is to demonstrate over and over again that problems we are given which at first don't seem easy or even possible to solve *can* be solved. If we solve these seemingly insolvable problems enough times, we develop faith that we will solve new ones that come along no matter how daunting they may at first seem. Life can be like that. People who get through some very trying times develop faith that they can handle whatever comes their way in the future.

Faith can take many different forms. It can be:

- faith in our own competence or ability
- faith that we will find a way or a resolution
- faith that it will somehow work out
- faith that we can handle the outcome no matter what it is
- faith that our natural state is a healthy one and it will come back if we lose it
- faith in God or an intelligence or power greater than us

Why does faith impact outcomes? How can faith improve our chances of success in overcoming a challenge? Faith as described here is not passive – it is not just "wait and hope." In fact, it is just the opposite: It is a very active process. But that accountable, proactive state can be short-circuited by our own thinking. One example is worried thinking. When we worry, we can become paralyzed, indecisive and immobile. If we are hopeful and believe there is a way, we tend to look for it and often find it. We see more options and discover more ways to be accountable to find a solution.

Optimism

Optimism is connected to faith and hope. It is a state of mind based on faith that things will turn out and answers can be found. And it can be learned.

Martin Seligman, PhD, is author of *Learned Optimism: Change Your Mind and Your Life*, and Director of the Positive Psychology Center at the University of Pennsylvania. He is founder of "positive psychology" (a branch of psychology which focuses on the empirical study of such things as positive emotions, strength-based character and healthy institutions).

Seligman's research has found that:

- optimists lead better quality and happier lives
- optimists live longer
- optimists are physically healthier
- optimists do better at work and in school
- optimists have less depression
- optimists have more friends, better relationships and better social lives

Seligman argues that the flip side of optimism is pessimism, which he relates to helplessness – the almost self-fulfilling belief that nothing you can do will matter, and that you are powerless.

One of the most interesting chapters in Seligman's book *Learned Optimism* concerns depression. He argues that the **negative thinking** that depressed people experience is not a symptom of depression – the thinking *is* the depression. Consequently, if you can change your thinking, you can cure the depression.

Studies have shown that people who have more optimistic thinking experience fewer and milder debilitating depressions. Research by Amy Farabaugh, PhD, of Massachusetts General

Hospital helps explain why and how optimism helps from a medical and clinical standpoint. In her research on optimism – defined as the tendency to believe that future goals and expectations can be met – she demonstrated that an optimistic state of mind was linked to physical well-being. There was a correlation between optimism and a stronger immune system, lower levels of cardiovascular inflammation, greater psychological resiliency, better mental heath and a longer life span.

"That is not a surprising finding," Farabaugh said, "because our attitudes can help determine our emotions and behaviors, which in turn determine our mental and physical states." She goes on to explain that more hopeful and optimistic people interpret the world differently than those caught up in negative thought. Optimists are more likely to feel they have more control over events, are less easily discouraged and more apt to persevere when facing difficulties. This makes them more likely to succeed. The pattern becomes self-reinforcing.

> "Optimism is the faith that leads to achievement. Nothing can be done without hope and confidence."
>
> – Helen Keller

It was that state of mind that enabled Helen Keller to impact the world despite her overwhelming handicaps. She was deaf and blind since early childhood, and lived in an era where most individuals similarly afflicted were consigned to an asylum. She overcame her disabilities and rose to international renown as an American lecturer, author and activist. She purposely used her fame to educate others about the blind and to raise funds for related charities.

Faith and hope leads to higher-quality thinking that in turn helps us find the way out of difficulties.

We have access to what I would call universal intelligence – those wonderful flashes of insight we sometimes get. If you have ever had a great outside-the-box idea or solution, or a brilliant thought and said to yourself in amazement, *Where did that come from?* then you know what I mean.

While faith can be personal and self-generated, it is most often referred to in a spiritual or religious context. It is a belief in a higher power or higher intelligence without what could be classically called proof.

Faith played a roll in my making it through college. I went off to engineering school right after Russia sent Sputnik (the first artificial satellite) into space. It was a time when it seemed like every kid in America wanted to be an engineer. Schools like the University of California at Los Angeles (UCLA) were inundated with engineering applications. They set up extremely high acceptance standards and still had to wash out two-thirds of the freshman class. I went from being a top student in my small high school to feeling like one of the dumbest of the exceptionally brainy kids in my class at UCLA.

I can still remember the calculus class that started at noon – with the bells of Royce Hall tolling ominously in the background. One day, our elderly and stern professor ordered me to the blackboard to solve a complex problem just after the bell stopped ringing. "Senn – problem three in the homework." As I struggled to solve the equation, he was right behind me erasing my work and shaking his head left to right. He then stopped me and suggested I consider changing my major or dropping the class.

I went home that weekend and told my mother I didn't think I could make it. She sat me down and talked to me in a very supportive and affirming way. She said I had all the God-given qualities I needed to succeed in school – and in life. I had been created whole, complete and capable. I just had to believe I could do it.

She told me something else that has stuck with me ever since that day. It was, I believe, her paraphrase of a biblical quote: *If you but have the faith of a grain of mustard seed.* I learned later the quote referred to the black mustard, a large annual plant that grows up to nine feet tall from a very tiny seed. If it could do that, couldn't I have faith I could handle school?

My mother also told me that the only thing that could stop me was my own thinking. She gave me a little book called *As a Man Thinketh* by James Allen. Originally published in 1902, it held wisdom from the ages. It begins with the following passage:

> "Mind is the Master power that molds and makes, and Man is Mind, and evermore he takes the tool of Thought, and, shaping what he wills, brings forth a thousand joys, a thousand ills: he thinks in secret, and it comes to pass: environment is but his looking-glass."
>
> – James Allen

I took what my mother had revealed to me and what I read in Allen's book as "I could do it if I believed I could." I just needed to have faith in a higher power and in myself, and be careful of my thoughts and self-talk.

I carried Allen's little book around for years. Other useful quotes I took from his book included:

"Every action and feeling is preceded by a thought."

"Right thinking begins with the words we say to ourselves."

"Circumstance does not make the man, it reveals him to himself."

I did finish engineering school, but concluded through some career testing that my passion wasn't in engineering – it was with people and in business. I went on to get my MBA, fell in love with solving business case studies and knew I wanted a career in consulting.

Realistic or Optimistic?

Some people reading this may say, "But I am *intentionally* more pessimistic because I believe it is important to be realistic." It is important to be realistic and to acknowledge reality even if it is not pretty – that is true. The question to examine once you have realistically assessed a challenging situation is: Where does your thinking go? Do you consume your energy worrying about the projected negative outcomes? Do you focus too much on why it won't work? Are the difficulties in the foreground rather than the possibilities? If so, pessimism is not serving you.

It is also important to know what optimism is *not*. It is not about the power of positive thinking. We will all ride the Mood Elevator from top to bottom and can't always have positive thoughts. What we *can* do is pay attention to our feelings as our guide to the quality of our thinking. If we can hold our pessimistic thoughts more lightly and take them less seriously, they will have less power over us and we will function better.

Another thing optimism is not is being naïve or a Pollyanna. There is a wise Sufi saying: "Trust in God and tie your camel." In other words, have faith and hope – but at the same time be realistic, plan contingencies, be prepared, proactive and accountable. The difference is in the mindset and the "come from."

Healthy optimism does not mean getting carried away with exuberance and unbridled excitement. A little-known secret of the Mood Elevator is that when we are overly excited and wildly enthusiastic, our thinking is also unreliable. Who hasn't acted impulsively or purchased something from a late night infomercial? Just as it is best not to make decisions when you are low on the Mood Elevator, it is also important not to make decisions when you are euphoric with an over-active mind. That has led to many spur-of-the-moment Las Vegas weddings that didn't work out and Hawaiian and Mexican timeshares and condos purchased on vacation.

Strange as it may seem, from the standpoint of "quality of thinking," wild enthusiasm goes on the Mood Elevator right next to anger. Both are intense feelings. Both are very compelling. Both are accompanied by a loud internal "voice" which justifies the action you want to take. The phenomenon is so well recognized that there are "grace periods" in most states before contracts become valid for new car purchases, mortgage re-finances and door-to-door sales of big ticket items – all items we can get too hyped about.

It is not hard to tell the difference between true higher mood states (like gratitude, wisdom and hopefulness) and from the dangers of elation. The difference is in our feelings. Excessive exuberance is a hyper feeling accompanied by a busy and of-ten spinning mind. Faith, hope and genuine optimism such as gratitude and other higher mood state feelings described in this book create a more serene feeling – the product of a qui-eter mind.

Few things can enhance our experience of life more than faith and hope. We all will face challenging situations and chal-lenging people in our lives. The healthiest and least stressful way to deal with them is to always include a good measure of faith and hope. So wherever that comes from for you, cherish it and nourish it, even in the most difficult times. It will serve you well.

Chapter Twenty-One

■■■■■■■■■■■■■■■

[your guide to riding the Mood Elevator]

iving life up the Mood Elevator and at your best is based on a few fundamental premises. Of all creatures on earth, man has been given the gift of thought. Along with that came consciousness and the ability to experience feelings, which are generated by our thoughts. It is through these gifts that we experience life.

Life happens, and it's not always pretty, but we have the choice to make of life what we will through our *thinking*. The power is ours; and so the first premise of living life up the Mood Elevator is to understand that our thinking creates our experience of life – and we are the thinker.

The second premise is that we came into this world with what could be called innate health. That includes the whole "system" that gives us the ability to experience life through our thoughts and feelings. It also represents a set of built-in, inborn (i.e., God-given) traits. These include the fact that we are naturally loving, curious and wise. Our innate health represents all the higher levels of the Mood Elevator.

Over time, we all develop "thought habits" and unhealthy-normal thinking that takes us away from our natural state. This is inevitable because our thinking creates our feelings – and our thinking varies from moment to moment and can be influenced by many things.

The points in this book are designed to help connect you to your innate health – the best of who you already are at your core. In some sense, you don't have to learn anything other than to access that innate health.

But to do that requires an understanding of the role of thought and the feelings that generates. Only *you* can learn to ride the Mood Elevator in your own unique way, just as only you could learn to walk beginning with those first few wobbly steps as a baby. The pointers introduced in this book will help you do just that. They are to:

1. Know that at your core you have innate health and the ability to be at your best. That is a very reassuring thing.

2. Know that to be human means you will ride the Mood Elevator and visit each and every floor.

3. Look to your feelings as your guide to tell you when you are down the Mood Elevator. Carry the Mood Elevator pocket card as a daily reminder.

4. Learn to recognize the feelings that accompany any unhealthy normal thinking or thought patterns, and make them a loud bell.

5. Know that your thinking is unreliable in the lower mood states, so delay, don't act on it – and don't take it out on others.

6. Live in the world of mild preference, not a world of "have-to's" and "my ways."

7. Take better care of yourself and remember to stretch and recover with exercise, sleep and time off.

8. Count your blessings daily and be grateful for life itself – maintain a gratitude perspective.

9. Stay connected to a higher purpose. Beware when the movie is "all about you."

10. Try pattern interrupts – change your thinking, change your feelings.

11. Have faith that, when you are down the Mood Elevator, this too shall pass – just like the weather. The sun is always up there; the clouds can obscure it but they will pass, as will your low mood.

There is a song called "Get Together" that was first made popular by the folk rock band The Youngbloods in the 1960s (and later used in a public service radio announcement as a call for brotherhood by the National Conference of Christians and Jews). It also has been featured in several films, including *Forrest Gump*. The repeating chorus to the song is:

C'mon people now,

Smile on your brother

Ev'rybody get together

Try and love one another right now

One of the verses speaks to the key we each hold to lead a more fulfilling life:

If you hear the song I sing,

You must understand

You hold the key to love and fear

All in your trembling hand

Just one key unlocks them both

It's there at your command

I believe that key is understanding the role of thought and knowing it is our own thinking that takes us up and down the Mood Elevator.

The greatest gift I received as a child was the message from my mother that my natural state was to be loving, wise and capable: that I was born whole and complete, and any time I doubted that, it was just an error in my thinking. My goal is to "pay it forward." My hope is that the thoughts in this book can put you on a path to finding that key and creating more love, joy, peace, inspiration, fulfillment and success in your life. ■

activities and information

creating your own Mood Elevator

The Mood Elevators in this book are a composite of input from thousands of people. In reality, we each have our own unique Mood Elevator, because we each have our own unique thought patterns. This section provides guidelines for you to create your own Mood Elevator.

Senn Delaney has seen hundreds of personalized versions of the Mood Elevator, from sessions where we ask people to make a list of the kinds of feelings they have when they are at their best and at their worst. As people share their "best" lists, there are commonalities. People at their best tend to feel more energetic, more lighthearted, more creative, more confident, more patient and understanding, happier and more optimistic. They tend to have a better sense of humor, don't take things as personally and feel they can pretty well handle whatever life has to offer.

Because there are times for all of us when we are at our worst, we also ask people to make a list of their feelings during down times, too. These lists include: low energy, being less confident, feeling less secure, less peaceful, more worried, more alone, stressed, impatient and bothered. When at their worst, people say that life can look overwhelming at times.

Some of the things on my list when I am at my worst include being more impatient, more intense, more easily bothered, worrying more, being less optimistic about outcomes and less creative and resourceful. Others say they become more angry, depressed, insecure, pessimistic, defensive, self-righteous and close-minded. Which, if any, of these mood states do you identify with?

As you personalize this notion of the Mood Elevator for yourself, think about times you had a really bad day. You would recognize those times by how the world looked to you; by the way you felt about people and things. Your job, your life conditions, even your loved ones didn't look as good to you. You might have felt worried, impatient, angry, insecure or less resourceful. Your thinking was not clear, and you were less effective. You weren't at your best because you were momentarily stuck.

You were visiting one of the lower floors on your own Mood Elevator.

You also have times, whether days or moments, when you are at your best – when you are operating at the "top of your game." Though you may be facing similar challenges as before, you have different inner feelings than when you are on the lower floors. You somehow believe you can handle the situation, no matter what it is. You feel more hopeful and optimistic. Your thoughts are clearer, and you are more creative and resourceful.

You are operating on the top floors of your Mood Elevator.

When you are at your best, do you feel more hopeful and optimistic? Are you more patient and a better listener? Do you have a better sense of humor? Are you less selfish and more understanding, compassionate and loving toward others? All of these are common experiences of people who are operating on the higher floors of their own Mood Elevator.

The list of feelings that you jot down when you are at your best and your worst will become your own personal Mood Elevator. They are feelings that run the full gamut – from gratitude to depression – that you experience based upon your thinking. Here is how to create your own Mood Elevator.

Down Your Mood Elevator

To get you started creating your own Mood Elevator, we will begin with the lower floors and then bring you back up to the higher floors.

On the next page is a more exhaustive list of feelings that may ring true for you when you are down the Mood Elevator and feeling at your worst. Your list may be different than this, but the mood states may provide you with clues. As you think about the list, transfer those most familiar to you to your own list on the page after next where you'll find your own Mood Elevator. Add those that occur to you that are not on this list. As much as possible, put the lowest of your feelings – perhaps like depression or anger – toward the bottom and the less intense ones higher up.

Up Your Mood Elevator

Next is a more complete list of people's feelings when they are on the upper floors of the Mood Elevator and feeling at their best. Place those that are most familiar and cherished by you at the top – things like love or peace or gratitude and then work your way down from there adding any that have meaning for you that are not shown here.

Once you have created your own Mood Elevator, you can use it as your personal guide. I'd also urge you to share it with friends and loved ones. It can be a reminder to you to remain more conscious and aware. It will also better assist you in knowing when and how to use the other pointers presented in this book.

Higher Mood State Feelings

Loving	Compassionate
Grateful	Understanding
Joyful	Caring
Happy	Supportive
Content	Wise
Peaceful	Creative
Inspired	Resourceful
Calm	Understanding
Generous	Productive
Patient	

Lower Mood State Feelings

Worried	Tense
Impatient	Frustrated
Irritable	Depressed
Bothered	Wound up
Judgmental	Overwhelmed
Insecure	Drained
Unworthy	Angry
Alone, lonely	Victimized
Sad	Misunderstood
Low energy	Judged
Low spirits	Mistreated

My Mood Elevator

At My Best – Top of my Game

_____

_____

_____

_____

_____

_____

At My Worst – Off my Game

_____

_____

_____

_____

_____

_____

the story behind the book

The acknowledgements page that follows this section gives credit to those who have had an impact on this book. It doesn't tell the story of where the concepts in the book came from and the role different people played. This section is for anyone who has an interest in that story.

Many of the notions in this book came to me through the school of life. That is, I learned them by reflecting on personal life experiences and from the work Senn Delaney has done to create Thriving organizational cultures for clients around the world. Other notions are my personal interpretation of concepts I've learned from some very progressive teachers in the field of mental health who first discovered and translated these principles.

Almost 20 years ago, Paul Nakai (a respected friend) asked my wife, Bernadette, and I to attend a lecture by a gentleman named Sydney Banks. Syd is the person I consider the originator of the core principles underlying the concepts in this book. He was a simple tradesman who one day had an epiphany. He had a flash of insight about the fact that his entire experience of life was a result of his thinking. He was touched by the notion that man was given the power of thought through which to experience life – and that we experienced it largely through our feelings or consciousness.

Syd had a simple but very touching way of communicating these profound notions and began to attract a following. My wife and I attended his one-day presentation on the campus of the University of California at Berkeley. It was nothing more than two, two-hour segments, with ample breaks, where Syd sat in a chair and talked about three principles: mind, consciousness and thought. Though we didn't fully grasp it (in fact, we didn't intellectually understand much of it!), we did come away from the lecture seeing life a little differently. We also felt noticeably different. We had an improved experience of life for many weeks afterwards: We were more patient, tolerant, peaceful and loving. Life somehow just looked better.

We were struck by the fact that people who had begun to understand these principles at a deeper level were reporting better relationships with family and loved ones, increased creativity, improved peace of mind, new resourcefulness, greater career effectiveness and more gratitude for life.

My wife (who at the time was head of Human Resources, including training and development for Senn Delaney), concluded that there might be some concepts in Syd's message that could help us in our work with clients. Senn Delaney's goal has always been to create healthy, high-performance teams and organizational cultures. An important aspect of that work are the seminars we conduct to connect our clients to a set of essential values and principles for life effectiveness. Bernadette reasoned that this might be another avenue to connect people to the best of who they really are.

At about the same time, we were introduced to another health-care professional, George S. Pransky, PhD, who had also become intrigued with Syd Bank's message. George made the decision to give up his traditional practice as a psychologist in the San Francisco Bay area and move to a small town north of Seattle to start a mental health practice to help individuals understand Syd's concepts.

If Bernadette and I were ever going to teach these principles, we had to learn to use them ourselves. So we decided to spend a week with George to see what we could learn. What was interesting was that he had developed a wellness practice rather than a *mental illness* practice. Most psychotherapy is about "fixing people." George's practice (and our goal) was to take people who were already successful by the world's standards and help them be even more effective and lead more fulfilling lives.

I began thinking about what might make me even more effective. What would enhance my experience of life? At the time, things were going quite well. Senn Delaney was successful. My kids were doing fine. My relationship with Bernadette, while not perfect, was very good – and improving with every year.

Upon reflection, there were definitely things that did detract from my effectiveness and my quality of life. One opportunity I was aware of is that I was wound pretty tight. I took my work and most everything else too seriously. I had a very busy mind and lived at a high level of impatience and intensity on what I know today as the Mood Elevator.

Occasionally, when I would take a vacation that lasted more than a week and allow my mind the time to quiet down, I would catch a glimpse of a very different kind of life – one where I was more appreciative of nature and of people, where I was in the present moment more often, where I was a better listener, where I experienced greater peace. But those moments were fleeting and the exception. As a result, I wasn't always the best listener – and in my haste to move forward, I would often finish other people's sentences. That was definitely something I could work on.

Another aspect of my life I realized I could work on that was even more compelling (and more draining), was what I now understand to be my "worry" habit. Even though my life was going quite well, I had a tendency to fill my mind too often with thoughts of worry.

Worry became the perfect topic, because worry is the ideal example of how we live through our thinking. When we worry about something and start spinning all our scenarios, it's as if the event really did happen. We have all of the physical, psychological and emotional consequences of the event – but the event hasn't actually occurred.

In reality, the vast majority of what we worry about never happens, and the things that do are rarely as significant as we make them out to be in our own minds. That got me to thinking how much better my quality of life would have been if I'd merely not worried about those things that never ended up happening. I urge you to ponder that same thought.

Our Blind Spots Need a Loud Bell

My time with George Pransky proved invaluable; it showed me that feelings of worry and Intensity were so much a part of my habit that they were a blind spot for me. Since I didn't notice them, I couldn't do much about them. As a result of my newfound understanding I began to value a quieter mind and more peaceful feelings. Feelings of excessive intensity and worry became more like "loud bells" – and those unhealthy thought habits diminished greatly.

As a result of continuing to deepen my understanding of the role of thought and incorporating the principles I learned from George into my life, I'm happy to report that today, I have a far more peaceful life with far less intensity and worry. I've become acutely aware of the feelings that go along with worry, so I recognize them when I go there on the Mood Elevator. Sometimes all it takes to snap me out of worry is a simple, gentle admonition to myself, such as "there you go again." This reminds me to be accountable for possible outcomes but not to create a soap opera in my head about it.

That early work with George, coupled with what I have learned since, has led me to the kind of relationship with my wife that is beyond what I could have imagined. It is continually fresh, loving, supportive, forgiving, stress free, passionate yet amazingly peaceful.

The impact these concepts have had on our five children, however, may be the most powerful gift I have received. That gift – and a desire to help others live life at their best – has led to my journey to create the Mood Elevator as a tool, and to discover the secrets of riding it better.

This positive personal experience set me on the path to better understand how to utilize these principles in my own life – and also incorporate them in the work Senn Delaney does with leaders and businesses around the world. It took years of trial and error in coaching leaders and leading seminars to find easy ways to help people understand the Mood Elevator and how to better ride it. It took additional years to explore some of the research and science governing our moods and to write this book. Today the Mood Elevator has become a foundational aspect of our corporate seminars. It is an integral part of the sessions we conduct to support personal change – which is one aspect of shaping an organization's culture.

In doing this work with organizations, the Mood Elevator has been embraced by employees from the CEO to front-line associates in more than 100 of the Fortune 500 organizations in the U.S. and dozens of Global 1000 firms around the world. We also have had great acceptance of the concept by major institutions like universities, hospitals and city and state governments. People from most every nation, language and level easily relate to the Mood Elevator and are able to use it as a guide to enhance their own lives.

In the last five years, we have found simple, common sense ways to connect people to the principles and give them practical pointers to riding the Mood Elevator with greater ease. We have also developed a large body of knowledge about the things that can (and do) affect our moods. People who use these pointers report they are able to live life at their best more often with more success and less stress. This book has been written to bring a deeper understanding to those who have some familiarity with the concept through our seminars and to introduce the Mood Elevator to a far broader audience as well.

acknowledgements

More people than I can mention here have helped keep me up the Mood Elevator, helped me understand the principles underlying it and provided life lessons in its use.

If I am to start where my understanding first began, I must thank most my mother, whom we all called Nana. She told me over and over again at a very young age that the feelings that are up the Mood Elevator – like love, self-confidence and wisdom – were God-given gifts that I was born with, and only error in my thinking could keep me from them.

Some of my greatest life lessons over the last 40 years have come from raising my five wonderful children: Kevin, Darin, Jason, Kendra and Logan. They continue to teach me about unconditional love, caring, a purpose beyond myself, being present and the joy of life through the eyes of a child.

My companion, soul mate and guide in learning about the concepts underlying the Mood Elevator is my wife, Bernadette. She helps me live them every day and understands them better than I do.

Bernadette, along with Paul Nakai, introduced me to Sydney Banks, the originator of the three principles that explain the Mood Elevator, and to George and Linda Pransky of Pransky and Associates, who first taught those principles to Senn Delaney and to me.

I would like to thank Jim Hart, Senn Delaney's CEO, as well as the other partners, consultants and staff at Senn Delaney including my assistant of over 30 years, Judy Gesicki, for supporting me in this effort. One of my partners Nick Neuhausel and his wife Laura helped me clarify my personal purpose which prompted me to complete the book. Special thanks to our Product Development team including Darin Senn for his creative ideas, Peter Brown and Paul Diniakos for layout graphics and cover design and contributing editor Susanne Stoeckeler Kuznetsky for her work on the final edits.

Larry Senn
Sunset Beach, California
January 2013

about the author

L arry Senn, DBA is a father, grandfather, husband, Sunday school teacher, best-selling author, lecturer, culture consultant, CEO coach and fitness enthusiast. He is chairman and founder of Senn Delaney, widely known as *The Culture-Shaping Firm.*

Dr. Senn has been referred to in business journals as "the father of corporate culture." His early experience in running a traditional consulting firm led him to conclude that all too many organizations were not reaching their full potential because of organizational habits, including trust issues, turf issues, blaming and excuses, lack of engagement, lack of customer focus, lack of agility and lack of positive spirit.

He saw that those habits of well-intentioned individuals reduced both the spirit and performance of even the best of organizations. It made the companies less fulfilling places to work, and made getting results harder than need be.

That realization inspired the first field research ever conducted on the concept of corporate culture – Larry's doctoral dissertation published in 1970. It led him to an early personal vision of finding a way to enhance the lives of people, the effectiveness of teams and the spirit and performance of organizations. That vision became Senn Delaney.

Since organizational transformation requires personal transformation, concepts and processes were developed that touched individuals. Participants in the Senn Delaney process have found that the concepts of leadership effectiveness were also useful principles of life effectiveness.

The Mood Elevator was one of those concepts. It, along with Be Here Now another Senn Delaney concept, became the two most universally embraced, retained and utilized by people in their lives at work and at home. To date, over one million people in 40 countries around the world have been exposed to the Mood Elevator. Those people have been a part of the Senn Delaney culture-shaping process in organizations of all kinds, from business corporations to hospitals, from schools and universities to governments at all levels.

Senn Delaney's vision today is:

To positively impact the world by inspiring leaders to create thriving cultures, which enhance the spirit and performance of organizations.

This book has been written to better support all the people who have been exposed to Senn Delaney processes, and to take the concept of the Mood Elevator to individuals worldwide, beyond Senn Delaney's client organizations. It is one part of fulfilling Larry's personal purpose which is:

To provide inspiration and understanding to an ever widening circle of people to live life "At Their Best" mentally, emotionally, physically and spiritually.

Dr. Senn lives in Sunset Beach, California, with his wife, Bernadette, and their 12-year-old son Logan mentioned often in the book. They have a daughter, Kendra, who is CEO and founder of a wellness/fitness business, The Fit Life (www.the-fitlife.com). They also have three older sons (Kevin, Darin and Jason), as well as five grandchildren. Kevin is a world-class kite surfer who owns Surf and Sail, a retail business on the North Shore of Oahu in Hawaii; Darin is Vice President, Creative Director at Senn Delaney; Jason runs Endless Summer Surf Camps around the world (www.endlesssummersurfcamp.com) and was part of the gold-medal-winning Team USA at the World Masters Surfing Championship in El Salvador.

The Senn's have a deep commitment to fitness and well-being. Bernadette is a competitive runner, and Larry runs, bikes and swims, competing in half a dozen triathlons a year.

For more information please visit:

www.upthemoodelevator.com

www.senndelaney.com

or contact:

larry@upthemoodelevator.com

index

A

B

C

H

J

K

L

M

N

O

P

Q

R

S

T

Y

notes

notes

notes